Big Book of
Family Meals

Reprinted in 2011
First published in 2009 by
New Holland Publishers (UK) Ltd
London • Cape Town • Sydney • Auckland

Garfield House
86–88 Edgware Road
London W2 2EA
www.newhollandpublishers.com

80 McKenzie Street
Cape Town 8001
South Africa

Unit 1, 66 Gibbes Street
Chatswood NSW 2067
Australia

218 Lake Road
Northcote
Auckland
New Zealand

10 9 8 7 6 5 4 3 2

ISBN 978 1 84773 549 2

Editor: Amy Corstorphine
Design: NHA and Vanessa Green
Production: Laurence Poos
Editorial Direction: Rosemary Wilkinson

Reproduction by Pica Digital Pte Ltd, Singapore
Printed and bound in India by Replika Press Pvt. Ltd

Publisher's note
The information given in this book is not intended as a
substitute for professional medical care. The publisher and
authors do not represent or warrant that the use of recipes
or other information contained in this book will necessarily
aid in the prevention or treatment of any disease, and
specifically disclaim any liability, loss or risk, personal or
otherwise, incurred as a consequence, directly or indirectly,
of the use and application of any of the contents of this
book. Readers must assume sole responsibility for any diet,
lifestyle and/or treatment programme that they choose to
follow. If you have questions regarding the impact of diet
and health, you should speak to a healthcare professional.

The publishers have made every effort to ensure that the
information contained in this book was correct at the time of
going to press, but medical and nutritional knowledge are
constantly evolving. The authors and publisher cannot be
held liable or responsible for any form of misuse of any herb,
herbal preparation or so-called herbal remedy. You should
check with a qualified medical practitioner that the product
is suitable for you.

Big Book of
Family Meals

130 inspiring recipes from around the world

NEW
HOLLAND

Contents

Introduction 6

Soups and starters 30

Mains – Meat 84

Fish 138

Veggie 192

Desserts 246

Index 300

Introduction

A well-balanced diet will keep you and your whole family healthy. Those who eat a healthy, varied diet are more likely to be full of energy, suffer fewer illnesses and children will be more attentive at school. Children grow rapidly between the ages of five and 12, gaining an average of 5–7.5 cm (2–3 in) in height each year. To support this rapid growth and development, they need a good supply of nutrients, especially protein, calcium and iron. It's not just the body that needs good nourishment, though. Many nutrients, especially the B vitamins and iron, are important for concentration and learning at work or school, and our brains needs a constant supply of glucose and oxygen. Teenagers have higher nutritional needs than any other group, yet often have the poorest diet, choosing the easy option of processed and fast foods. Encouraging good food habits from an early age could have a significant effect on health throughout adolescence and throughout life, and could help protect against problems such as osteoporosis, heart disease and some cancers.

The recipes in this book are about striking a balance between healthy eating and food that the whole family will enjoy. Eating well shouldn't mean boring meals or denying favourite foods, but rather providing a diet that is healthy and varied, as well as delicious.

So much has been written in the past decade about what we shouldn't eat that most of us are well aware that too many sugary, fatty, or over-processed foods should be avoided. But healthy eating is not about deprivation; the secret lies in serving more foods that will promote wellbeing and that everyone will enjoy.

Fruit and vegetables

These are packed with vitamins and minerals and 'phytochemicals', which help to keep the immune system strong and protect against everyday illnesses. To ensure your family gets a wide variety of these nutrients, try to include as many different coloured fruits and vegetables as you can.

Both adults and children should aim for at least five portions a day. Fresh, frozen, tinned and dried fruit and vegetables and 100 per cent juice, all count. An adult-size portion could be three heaped tablespoons of cooked carrots, peas or sweetcorn, a medium-sized apple, pear or banana, three heaped tablespoons of canned fruit salad, a fruity cereal or snack bar, a few dried apricots or a tablespoon of dried fruit such as raisins. Child-size portions should be slightly smaller.

Easy ways to eat more fruit and vegetables

- Start the day with a glass of fruit juice at breakfast or top cereals with chopped fresh or dried fruit.
- Serve crunchy vegetable sticks as a snack with favourite dips.
- Stir a handful of frozen peas or mixed vegetables into soups and casseroles before serving.
- Purée vegetables into sauces or blend with a little stock and milk to make nutritious soups.
- Make a pot of 'trail mix' from dried fruit, nuts and seeds to lunch boxes and for sprinkling over yoghurts and desserts.

Calcium and iron-rich foods

Vitamins and minerals are complex substances needed by the body for a whole range of processes. All are important, but of particular note to families with young children are the minerals iron and calcium. Iron, often lacking in children's diets, is needed for both mental and physical development and to make haemoglobin, which transports oxygen around the body. Iron is especially important for girls who need to build up supplies as they approach puberty. Make sure that your child has at least one iron-rich food every day.

Calcium is vital for building strong healthy bones and teeth. It also acts as a 'bone bank', helping to build up bone density from an early age to reduce the risk of osteoporosis later in life. Vitamin D is vital for the absorption and utilisation of calcium. As this vitamin isn't well absorbed from food, the best way to get adequate supplies is to spend a few minutes outside everyday, especially on sunny days, but avoid staying out for long in the middle of the day, when the sun is at its hottest.

Omega 6 and omega 3

Although we tend to think of all fats as being 'bad', some actually play a protective role in the diet and two in particular are vital: the essential fatty acids (EFAs) known as omega 6 and omega 3. Omega 6 EFAs are involved in the production of prostaglandin, a hormone-like substance needed for healthy cell membranes which has a therapeutic effect on skin problems and allergies. They are found in many oils including sunflower and safflower, soft polyunsaturated margarine, seeds and nuts. Omega 3 EFAs are also found in these oils but additionally include vital substances which come almost solely from fish oils. Vegetarians may get small amounts from flax and pumpkin seeds and leafy green vegetables, although recent evidence suggests that the type of fatty acids found in vegetable sources may not have the same benefits as those in fish. Omega 3 EFAs help to support healthy brain development and there is evidence that they may influence a child's ability to learn and concentrate. Scientists are still studying whether omega 3 can help with conditions such as Attention Deficit Hyperactivity Disorder (ADHD) and other mental illnesses such as depression.

Try to make sure that the whole family eats oily fish such as salmon, tuna or sardines at least once a week. If someone in your family doesn't like fish, there are plenty of polyunsaturated spreads and yoghurt drinks enriched with omega 6 and omega 3.

Sugar

Most of us enjoy sugary foods and eating them occasionally causes no real harm. When children grow older, outside influences will make themselves felt and you will no longer have complete control over what is eaten. In fact, a staggering 80 per cent of children eat more added sugars than the maximum level recommended for adults. But while sugars occur naturally in foods such as milk and fruit, it's the food containing added sugar that you should try to reduce in your family's diet, including sweets, cookies, cakes and pastries, fizzy and juice drinks. Not only do they contribute to tooth decay, high-sugar foods raise blood sugar levels quickly, causing peaks and troughs of energy. A sugary snack may give you instant energy, but this will be followed by a dip and these fluctuations in blood sugar levels cause mood swings and affect attentiveness. When checking food labels, watch out for other words for sugar, including sucrose, glucose, fructose, maltose, corn syrup, hydrolysed starch and invert sugar.

Ways to cut down on sugar

- Eat fewer sugary sweets and snacks. If your children can't avoid the sweet shop, encourage better choices such as a small bar of chocolate.
- Instead of sugary juice drinks and canned fizzy drinks such as cola and lemonade, go for unsweetened fruit juice, preferably diluted with water. For a fizzy drink treat, try mixing fruit juice with carbonated water.
- Instead of reaching for the biscuit tin, try serving a brioche roll with a little good-quality jam, crunchy breadsticks or a toasted currant bun.
- Leave the sugar bowl off the breakfast table; sprinkling sugar on cereals should be avoided, as should sugar- and honey-coated kids' cereals.
- Instead of sugary yoghurts, mousses and trifles, offer plain 'bio' or Greek yoghurt with sliced fresh fruit or fruit purée.

Saturated and hydrogenated fats

While adults should aspire to eat a high-fibre, low-fat diet, this isn't ideal for children. They need a greater intake of fat than adults as it is a concentrated source of energy. Fat also helps the absorption of vitamins A, D, E and K, as well as calcium. It is, however, important to limit the amount of saturated fats as these raise the type of cholesterol in the blood that increases the risk of coronary heart disease – there is growing evidence that this starts in childhood. From the age of five, children can gradually start to include reduced-fat foods in their diet, such as semi-skimmed/low-fat milk. Hydrogenation is a process by which liquid oil is turned into solid fat. During the process, trans fats may be formed, which are thought to be more harmful than saturated fats. Always check labels and avoid foods containing hydrogenated fat or hydrogenated vegetable oil.

Ways to cut back on undesirable fats

- Limit foods containing high amounts of saturated fats such as butter, cream and foods made with them, including cakes, pastries and cookies.
- Cut down on 'visible' fats such as butter on bread, cream on desserts and always trim fat from meats such as chops and bacon.

- Choose margarines and spreads that contain little or no hydrogenated or saturated fats.
- Avoid fast food takeaways as these are usually fried in partially hydrogenated oil.
- Swap fatty snacks for healthy ones some of the time – for example, breadsticks instead of crisps or a slice of wholemeal toast with jam instead of biscuits or a sweet pastry.

Salt

Salt is made up of two components – sodium and chloride. It is sodium which leads to health problems; in excess, it can cause high blood pressure (hypertension), increasing the chances of heart attacks and strokes. It is also linked to an increased risk of osteoporosis and has been shown to aggravate asthma. People who eat too much salt when young often develop a taste for salty food and will be more likely to continue to eat too much salt when older. Most adults and children eat more than double the recommended daily maximum amount of salt. Children should have considerably less salt than adults. While obvious solutions include reducing the amount of salt used in cooking and not having extra salt on the table, about three-quarters of the salt we eat is already in the foods we buy. Many processed foods are high in salt and it's not always the obvious ones. Shop-bought bread, cakes and pastries, baked beans and sauces contain a surprising amount.

Some manufacturers have reduced the amount of salt in their products, so it's worth checking carefully when shopping. Most foods are labelled with the amount of sodium (rather than salt) they contain. If you want to compare a product labelled with its salt rather than sodium content, it's worth knowing that there's about 2.5 g of sodium in every 6 g of salt. Other types of sodium are used as preservatives or flavour enhancers, such as monosodium glutamate, often added to processed meats, snacks and soups.

Ways to cut down on salt
- Eat fewer salty foods including salted nuts, bacon, smoked fish and pickles. Don't add a bag of crisps to your lunchbox every day; go for low-salt snacks such as unsalted nuts and home-made popcorn.
- Be sparing with sauces, especially bottled and packet sauces, soy sauce, Worcestershire sauce, brown sauce and tomato ketchup. If you use these when cooking, reduce or omit additional salt.
- Make your own stock or choose lower-salt stock cubes and use herbs and spices to add flavour to cooking.
- Choose tinned vegetables and pulses without added salt.

- Compare labels to help you choose those with less added salt. Similar products often vary considerably in the amount of sodium they contain.
- Ask for unsalted fries and chips when eating out in restaurants or buying takeaways and make them an occasional treat only.
- Replace processed meats such as burgers and sausages with home-made versions.
- Do not use salt at the table. Always taste your food before automatically adding extra salt and encourage your children to do the same.

Dealing with food allergies

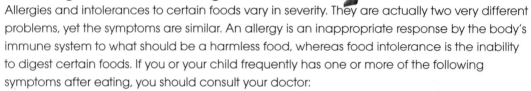

Allergies and intolerances to certain foods vary in severity. They are actually two very different problems, yet the symptoms are similar. An allergy is an inappropriate response by the body's immune system to what should be a harmless food, whereas food intolerance is the inability to digest certain foods. If you or your child frequently has one or more of the following symptoms after eating, you should consult your doctor:

- Nausea, abdominal pain, bloating, vomiting or diarrhoea.
- Swelling of the face, mouth or tongue.
- Wheeziness, streaming eyes and sneezing.
- Blotchy rashes, particularly on the face.
- Foods that can bring on allergies include nuts, seeds, fish and shellfish, egg white, berries and citrus fruit. Nuts (especially peanuts and brazils) are the most common of these and some schools ban these from all packed lunches to protect those children who may react even if they are only in the vicinity of nuts. Children under the age of three with a family history of allergy should not be given nuts in any form. Some children may have a severe (anaphylactic) reaction to certain foods, manifesting itself as difficulty with breathing, a very fast pulse rate and bluish skin or lips. In these cases immediate hospital treatment should be sought.

Food intolerances may be present at birth or may develop later in life. Lactose intolerance is the inability to digest the sugars in cow's milk. If you or your child suffers from this it will be necessary to follow a dairy-free diet in which soya or low-lactose milk products are used instead. Avoid foods labelled as containing milk, butter, margarine, cheese, yoghurt, cream, whey, casein/caseinates and lactose. If avoiding dairy products you will need to ensure an adequate intake of calcium and vitamins A and D.

Coeliac disease is a sensitivity to gluten, a protein found in cereals, including wheat, rye, barley and oats (it is also possible to have an intolerance just to wheat). More common in girls than boys, it often runs in families and can start at any age. It affects about one person in 130. There are many gluten-free products available, including breads and pasta.

Recipe accompaniments

Crispy pizza base

4 tsp dried granular yeast

300ml/10fl oz lukewarm
  water

500g/1lb 2oz plain flour

1 tsp salt

Makes 4 x 25–30cm/10–12in pizzas

Sprinkle the yeast into 100ml/3½ fl oz of the water. Leave to dissolve for 5–10 minutes. Add about 2 Tbsp of the flour and mix to a smooth paste then stir in the remaining water. Cover and leave the yeast mixture for about 30 minutes or until it is bubbling and foamy.

Combine the flour (reserve 2 Tbsp for kneading) and salt in a large bowl and make a well in the centre. Pour in the yeast liquid. Using a wooden spoon, work the ingredients together by pulling the flour into the liquid until it comes together. Use your hands to transfer the mixture to a lightly floured surface. Knead the dough for 10 minutes or until it is smooth and elastic. Form the dough into a round loaf. Leave to rise under a clean tea towel for about 1½–2 hours or until doubled in size.

Punch down the dough and knead for a couple of minutes. Divide into four balls. Press each dough ball out flat and, using a floured rolling pin, shape into a 25–30cm/10–12in diameter circle. Using your knuckles, press just inside the edges to raise them slightly. Leave to rest for 10–15 minutes. Preheat oven to 220°C/425°F/Gas mark 7.

Add your toppings. Cook in the middle of the oven for 10–12 minutes (unless otherwise instructed depending on the toppings) or until crispy and golden and the base is cooked.

Gluten-free quick pizza base dough

175g/6oz brown or white
 rice flour
1 Tbsp caster sugar
½ tsp bicarbonate of soda
½ tsp salt
225ml/8fl oz plain yogurt

Makes 2 x 30cm/12in thin crusts

Preheat the oven to 180°C/350°F/Gas mark 6. Combine the flour, sugar, bicarbonate of soda and salt in a large bowl. Add the yogurt and stir until roughly combined. Turn the dough on to a floured surface and knead for 1 minute, or until it comes together into a smooth ball. Form into two balls with your hands and transfer to a lightly floured surface.

   Flour a rolling pin and roll the dough to about 1cm/½in thick and 25cm/10in in diameter. Place onto a lightly floured baking sheet and top as required. Cook in the middle of the preheated oven for 12–15 minutes or until cooked and golden.

Quick scone base

250g/9oz plain
 (All purpose) flour
1 tsp baking powder
1 pinch salt
30g/1¼oz butter (at room
temperature), cut into cubes
200ml/7–9fl oz milk

Preheat the oven to 200°C/400°F/Gas mark 6. Sift and combine the flour, baking powder and salt in a large bowl. Add the cubes of butter and lightly rub into the flour until the mixture resembles the texture of breadcrumbs. Add the milk to the rubbed mixture and stir with a palette knife or metal spoon until it begins to come together. Finish it off with your hands – it should be soft but not sticky (if the dough seems too dry add a little more milk, a teaspoon at a time). The dough should come together and leave the sides of the bowl clean.

   Shape the dough into a ball with your hands and transfer it to a lightly floured surface. Flour a rolling pin and roll the dough out to about 1cm/½in thick and 25cm/10in in diameter.

   Place the round on a lightly floured baking sheet and top as required. Cook in the middle of the preheated oven for 12–18 minutes, depending on the topping, or until cooked and golden.

Focaccia pizza base

2 tsp dried granular yeast
250ml/9fl oz lukewarm water
500g/1lb 2oz plain flour
1 tsp salt
3 Tbsp olive oil

Makes 2 x 25cm/10in pizzas

Sprinkle the yeast into the water. Leave to dissolve for 5–10 minutes. Combine the flour (reserving about 2 Tbsp for kneading) and salt in a large bowl and make a well in the centre. Pour in the olive oil and yeasted water. Using a wooden spoon, work the ingredients together by pulling the flour into the liquid mixture until it comes together, adding a little additional water if necessary. Using your hands, transfer the mixture to a lightly floured surface. Knead the dough for 10 minutes or until it is smooth, silky and elastic in texture. Form the dough into a ball and put in a clean, lightly oiled bowl. Cover with a clean tea towel and leave to rise for about 1–1½ hours or until doubled in size.

Once doubled in size, knock the dough back and knead for a further 5 minutes. Cut the dough into two even-sized pieces, press out flat and, using a floured rolling pin, shape into about 25cm/10in rounds. Cover again and leave to rest for a further 15–20 minutes.

Preheat the oven to 220°C/ 425°F/Gas mark 7. Using the tips of your fingers, make shallow indentations all over the surface of the dough. The dough is now ready to be topped. Cook on a lightly floured baking sheet in the middle of the oven for 14–16 minutes or until golden and the base is cooked through.

Sweet honey pizza base

2 tsp dried granular yeast

125ml/4fl oz lukewarm water

175ml/6fl oz lukewarm full-
fat milk

175ml/6fl oz runny honey

1 Tbsp extra virgin olive oil

1 large egg, beaten

Finely grated zest of 1 lemon

8g/¼oz saffron powder
(optional)

1 tsp salt

550–600g/1lb 4oz–1lb 5oz
plain flour

Makes 2 x 30cm/12in thick-crust bases or 4 x 30cm/12in thin-crust bases

Sprinkle the yeast into the water. Leave to dissolve for 5–10 minutes. Add the milk, honey, oil, egg, lemon zest and saffron (if using) to the yeast mixture and stir well. Sift the salt and flour into the wet mixture and mix to a dough, adding additional flour if necessary to form a ball. Transfer the mixture to a lightly floured surface and knead for 10–15 minutes or until smooth and elastic. Return the dough to a clean bowl and leave covered for about 1½ hours or until doubled in size.

Knock the dough back and divide into two or four, depending on the desired thickness of the base required, and shape into 25–30cm/10–12in rounds. Leave the dough to rest for 10–15 minutes.

Preheat the oven to 220°C/425°F/Gas mark 7. Add your toppings. Cook the pizzas in the middle of the oven for 10–12 minutes for a thin base or 15–18 minutes for a thicker base or until lightly golden and crispy.

Egg pasta

200g/7oz plain flour
100g/4oz semolina flour
½ tsp salt
3 eggs
1 Tbsp olive oil

Serves 4

Place the flours and salt in a large bowl and mix together. Make a hollow reservoir in the centre and crack the eggs into it and add the oil. With a fork slowly break up the eggs and draw the flour in to make a paste. Keep going until all of the flour has been mixed in and it forms a ball. If it is too damp add a little more flour and if too dry add a little more water. Knead the dough until it is soft and silky and when you press your finger into it the depression bounces out. This will take about 10 minutes (but depends on how consistently you knead). Wrap the pasta in cling film and refrigerate for 30 minutes.

When it comes to rolling the pasta you can either use a pasta machine, following the directions supplied, or alternatively roll the dough on a lightly-floured work-surface using a rolling pin. Roll the pasta, turning occasionally, until it is thin enough for you to see your fingers through it. Leave the pasta to dry in sheets or cut into shapes as desired.

Chicken stock

1 uncooked chicken carcass
   or whole chicken about
   1kg/2lb 4oz)
3 bay leaves
1 tsp black peppercorns
2 celery sticks, leaves
   included, roughly chopped
2 carrots, unpeeled,
   chopped
1 onion, unpeeled, halved
3 sprigs thyme
2L/3pt cold water

All stock recipes make approximately 1.5L/2¾pt

Put all the ingredients in a large stockpot, adding extra water if necessary to ensure the chicken is covered by about 2.5cm/1in water. Bring to a gentle simmer and continue to simmer for about 1½–2 hours, skimming off any scum with a large spoon, as the stock simmers. Leave to cool slightly before straining through a fine sieve.

Meat stock

1kg/2lb 4oz meat bones,
   preferably veal or beef
1 onion, unpeeled, halved
3 bay leaves
1 tsp black peppercorns
2 celery sticks, leaves
   included, roughly chopped
1 carrot, unpeeled, chopped
2 tomatoes, chopped
2 sprigs rosemary
2L/3½pt cold water

Roast the bones in a dry roasting tin at 200°C/400°F/Gas mark 6 for about 40 minutes. Transfer to a large stockpot and add the remaining ingredients. Place the roasting tin, with a little hot water added, on the hob and heat, stirring until boiling. Boil for 2–3 minutes, scraping any of the sticky residue from the base and sides of the tin. Add this to the stockpot. Cover all the ingredients in the stockpot with water, adding extra if necessary to ensure that everything is covered by about 2.5cm/1in. Bring to a gentle simmer and simmer for about 1½–2 hours. Leave to cool slightly before straining through a fine sieve.

Vegetable stock

2 celery sticks, leaves
  included, chopped

2 leeks, roughly chopped

1 onion, unpeeled, halved

2 carrots, unpeeled,
  chopped

1 head garlic, cut in half
  horizontally

5 sprigs parsley

3 bay leaves

5 sprigs thyme or 1 bouquet
  garni

1 tsp black peppercorns

2L/3½pt cold water

Put all the ingredients in a large stockpot and cover with water, adding extra if necessary to ensure everything is covered by about 2.5cm/1in. Bring to a gentle simmer, removing any scum with a large spoon, and simmer for about 1 hour. Leave to cool slightly before straining through a fine sieve.

Tamarind purée

300g/11oz block compressed
  tamarind

about 700ml/24fl oz water

To use the tamarind block, soak it overnight in twice its volume of hot water. The next day pulp it well with the back of a spoon, then strain through a metal sieve, discarding the husks. The brown liquid should be quite thick, and there will be plenty of it. Freeze any spare. Alternatively for a small portion cut off about an eighth of the block – a piece about 4 cm/1½ in. Soak this in about 3½ fl oz/100 ml water for half an hour or more. Pulp and strain as above. More labour-intensive but better results can be achieved by boiling the block in plenty of water and then sieving it whilst hot. Remove the pulp and then boil again in fresh water and sieve as before. Repeat this process twice more.

Lemon or vinegar, which can be used as substitutes, will give completely different flavours.

Rocket pesto

60–80g/2¼–3oz rocket
  leaves

1 clove garlic, crushed

50g/2oz finely grated
  Parmesan cheese

50g/2oz pine nuts

150–200ml/7fl oz extra virgin
  olive oil

Sea salt and freshly ground
  black pepper to taste

Makes 250ml/8fl oz

Put the rocket, garlic, Parmesan and pine nuts in a food
processor with about a quarter of the olive oil. Whizz to
a coarse purée. With the motor still running, drizzle in
the remaining olive oil until the desired consistency is
reached. Season – Parmesan varies in saltiness so it is
important to taste the pesto before seasoning. Transfer
to an airtight container and cover with a thin layer of oil.
Seal and refrigerate for up to 2 weeks.

Walnut pesto

2 cloves garlic, peeled and
  roughly chopped

50g/2oz grated Parmesan
  cheese

100g/3½oz fresh shelled
  walnuts

125–150ml/4–5fl oz extra
  virgin olive oil

1 handful basil leaves, torn

Salt and freshly ground black
  pepper to taste

Makes 250ml/8fl oz

Put the garlic, Parmesan, walnuts and a good splash of
olive oil in a food processor and whizz to a paste. With the
motor still running, drizzle in the remaining olive oil until
the desired consistency is reached. Tear up the basil into
the food processor and blitz once or twice to combine
but do not whizz to completely purée the basil. Add salt
and pepper. Transfer to a jar or airtight container and
cover with a thin layer of olive oil. Seal and refrigerate for
up to 2 weeks.

Coriander pesto

2 cloves garlic, peeled and roughly chopped

3 Tbsp grated Parmesan cheese

25g/1oz fresh shelled walnuts

1 red chilli, halved, with stem and seeds removed

75ml/2½fl oz extra virgin olive oil

40g/1½oz coriander

10g/½oz mint

10g/¼oz chives

Grated rind of 1 lime

Juice of ½ lime

Salt and freshly ground black pepper to taste

Makes 250ml/8fl oz

Put the garlic, Parmesan, walnuts, chilli and 1 Tbsp of the olive oil in a food processor and whizz to a paste. With the motor still running, drizzle in the remaining olive oil until the desired consistency is reached. Add the herbs, lime rind and juice to the food processor and blitz to combine but do not whizz to completely purée the herbs. Add salt and pepper to taste. Transfer to a jar or airtight container and cover with a thin layer of oil. Seal and refrigerate for up to 2 weeks.

Croûtons

1 Tbsp olive oil

2 cloves garlic, crushed

1 baguette, cut into 1cm/½in diagonal slices

Makes about 24–36

Preheat the oven to 180°C/375°F/Gas mark 4. Combine the oil and garlic in a bowl and brush the mixture, using a pastry brush, over both sides of the bread slices. Place on a baking tray and bake for about 15–20 minutes or until crispy and golden.

These will keep in an airtight container for up to 3 weeks.

Tomato, black olive, garlic and basil salsa

4 beef tomatoes, finely
chopped

125g/4oz stoned black
olives in brine, drained and
finely chopped

2 cloves garlic, peeled and
finely chopped

Few sprigs fresh basil, finely
chopped

2 Tbsp extra virgin olive oil

2 Tbsp balsamic vinegar

Salt and freshly ground black
pepper

- Mix all the ingredients together, cover and chill until required.

Sweet and sour brown tamarind chutney

100g/4oz tamarind purée

50g/2oz dates, pitted

50g/2oz brown sugar

½ onion, chopped

1 teaspoon garam masala

chilli powder, to taste

black salt (kala namak) or
white sea salt, to taste

- Grind the ingredients in a blender or food processor, adding just enough water to make a smooth purée.

Thai chilli paste

3–4 bird's eye chillies, halved and deseeded

2 tsp coriander seeds, toasted

1 tsp cumin seeds, toasted

2–3 cardamom pods

2 shallots, peeled and finely chopped

2 garlic cloves, peeled and roughly chopped

2cm/¾in piece fresh root ginger, peeled and roughly chopped

3 kaffir lime leaves, central vein removed and finely shredded

2 Tbsp vegetable oil

1 tsp fish sauce

1 large handful fresh coriander leaves and stalks

soy sauce

Makes 4–5 Tbsp

Chop the dried chillies into 1cm/½in pieces and soak in warm (boiled) water until softened, about 20 minutes. Drain well.

Heat a small frying pan over high heat. Add the coriander seeds, cumin seeds and cardamom pods and toast until they pop and are fragrant, 2–3 minutes. Remove from the heat and cool. Grind in a mortar with a pestle.

Combine all of the remaining ingredients, except for the soy sauce, in a food processor and pulse until combined. Add enough soy sauce to make a slightly runny paste.

The paste is best the day it's made, but if you cover the surface directly with clingfilm it will keep in the fridge for up to one week.

White onion paste

1kg/2.2lb white onion, coarsely chopped

50ml/2fl oz vegetable oil

Makes about 400g/14oz when puréed

Fry or bake the onions until they caramelize. Blend the onions and their oil down to a purée using a little water as needed.

Basic savoury white sauce

45g/1½oz butter
45g/1½oz plain flour
600ml/20fl oz milk
**Salt and freshly ground black
  pepper**

Melt the butter in a saucepan, add the flour and stir until smooth. Cook gently for 2 minutes, stirring, until bubbling. Remove from the heat and gradually stir in the milk. Return to a moderate heat and bring to the boil, stirring continuously, and cook gently for about 3 minutes. Add seasoning to taste and serve.

   For a cheese sauce – add 125g/4oz grated mature Cheddar and ¼ tsp dry mustard powder.

   For a herb sauce – add 4 Tbsp assorted finely chopped herbs, such as parsley, chives or sage.

Quick classic tomato sauce

3 Tbsp tomato purée
1 tsp dried basil
1 tsp dried oregano
½ tsp caster sugar
½ tsp salt
½ tsp dried chilli flakes
½ tsp crushed black pepper
2 cloves garlic, finely
  chopped (optional)

Makes 500ml/18fl oz

Combine all ingredients in a food processor and blend until smooth. Transfer to a small bowl or measuring jug and use immediately, or cover and either refrigerate for up to 1 week or freeze.

Basic crêpe batter

125g/4oz plain flour

30g/1oz caster sugar
  (optional)

1 pinch salt

2 whole eggs

2 egg yolks

300ml/10fl oz milk

75g/2oz unsalted butter,
  melted

Makes 12 crêpes

Combine the flour, sugar, if using, and salt in a bowl. Make a well in the centre and break in the eggs then add the extra yolks. Add half the milk and gradually work into the flour using a whisk. Beat lightly until smooth, taking care not to over-mix.

Add the remaining milk gradually, whisking gently until well combined. Transfer to a jug, cover loosely and leave in a cool place for 30 minutes. Stir 60g/2oz melted butter into the batter before using.

Lightly brush a small frying pan – 15cm/6 in diameter base – with a little of the remaining butter and heat until hot. Holding the pan, pour in about 50ml/2fl oz batter and tilt the pan from side to side so that it runs into a thin, even layer across the bottom of the pan.

Place the pan over moderate heat and cook for about 1 minute, or until the crêpe browns around the edges and begins to curl away from the pan. Slide a palette knife under the crêpe and flip it over. Brown the underside for a further minute.

Turn out on to a wire rack lined with a clean tea towel and baking parchment. Fold the paper and towel over the crêpe to keep it moist. Continue to make a further 11 crêpes, brushing the pan with melted butter as necessary, gently stirring the batter each time it is used, and stacking the cooked crêpes between sheets of parchment, until you are ready to serve.

Basic pancake batter

125g/4oz plain flour
1 pinch salt
1 egg
300ml/10fl oz milk
Vegetable oil

Makes 8 pancakes

Combine the flour and salt in a bowl, make a well in the centre and break in the egg. Add half the milk and gradually work into the flour using a whisk. Beat lightly until well combined and smooth. Add the remaining milk gradually, whisking gently until the batter has the consistency of pouring cream. Transfer to a jug, cover loosely and leave in a cool place for 30 minutes. Never leave the batter longer than 1 hour, unless covered and refrigerated, otherwise it will start to ferment.

Lightly brush a medium frying pan – 20cm/8in diameter base – with vegetable oil and heat until hot. Pour away any excess oil – the pan should be practically dry. Holding the pan, pour in about 4 Tbsp batter into the middle of the pan then tilt the pan from side to side so the batter runs into a thin, even layer across the bottom of the pan.

Place the pan over moderate heat and cook for about 1½ minutes, or until the pancake browns around the edges and begins to curl away from the pan. Slide a palette knife under the pancake and flip it over. Brown the underside of the pancake for a further minute.

Turn the pancake out on to a wire rack lined with a clean tea towel and baking parchment. Fold the paper and towel over the pancake to keep it moist. Continue to make a further 7 pancakes, re-oiling the pan as necessary, and stacking the cooked pancakes between sheets of parchment, until you are ready to serve. Pancakes will keep warm like this while you cook the remaining batter, but if you want to keep them warm for longer, transfer them, still layered up, to a heatproof plate, cover with foil and place over a pan of gently simmering water or in the oven at a low (keep warm) setting.

Basic waffle batter

250g/8oz plain flour

½ tsp bicarbonate of soda

½ tsp salt

30g/1oz caster sugar
(optional)

1 egg, separated

300ml/10fl oz milk

30g/1oz unsalted butter,
melted

Makes 12 waffles

Prepare and preheat the waffle irons or waffle machine as directed. Combine the flour with the bicarbonate of soda, salt and sugar, if using, in a bowl and make a well in the centre. Add the egg yolk and milk, and gradually work into the flour using a whisk. Beat gently until smooth. Carefully stir in the melted butter.

In a grease-free bowl, whisk the egg white until stiff and carefully fold into the batter using a large metal spoon.

Pour over enough batter, to ensure that the moulded surface of the lower plates are covered sufficiently (for an electric plate you will need about 3 Tbsp for each plate). Close the irons or lid and cook until the waffles are just brown on the outside, about 3 minutes.

When the waffles are ready, remove them with a two-pronged fork or a wooden skewer, taking care not to scratch the non-stick coating. Place on a wire rack lined with a clean tea towel and baking parchment. Fold the paper and towel over the waffle to keep it moist. Continue to make waffles, about 12 in total, stacking the cooked waffles between sheets of parchment, until you are ready to serve.

Blueberry compôte

Juice of 1 orange

1 tsp cornflour

200g/7oz fresh blueberries

2 Tbsp caster sugar

Makes 300ml/10fl oz

Combine the orange juice and cornflour in a small bowl. Put the blueberries, sugar and cornflour mixture in a small saucepan over a low heat. Stir gently until the blueberries begin to macerate and their juice just starts to run. Stir gently for a further 30 seconds then remove from the heat and allow to cool. Store in the refrigerator for up to 1 week.

Fruit coulis

½ quantity Sugar syrup, without the cocoa powder (see opposite)

250g/8oz of any of the following: raspberries, blackberries, blueberries or strawberries, washed and prepared, or 1 large ripe mango or papaya, peeled, deseeded and chopped

1–2 Tbsp freshly squeezed lemon juice (optional)

Each coulis makes approx. 550ml/18fl oz

Make the syrup as described opposite and, once the syrup has cooked, add your chosen fruit to it before it cools.

Once cold, transfer to a blender or food processor and blend for a few seconds until smooth. Strain through a nylon sieve to make a smooth sauce. If the sauce is too sweet, add lemon juice to sharpen. Cover and chill until required.

You can try adding extra flavourings to your chosen coulis, such as finely grated citrus rind, vanilla extract or rosewater.

Chocolate sugar syrup

350g/12oz caster sugar
600ml/20fl oz cold water
1 Tbsp cocoa powder

Makes approx. 600ml/20fl oz

Place the sugar in a saucepan and pour in the water. Heat, stirring until the sugar dissolves. Raise the heat and bring to the boil. Simmer, without stirring, for 10 minutes. Remove from the heat. Sieve in the cocoa powder and whisk well. Set aside to cool.

Custard sauce

4 level Tbsp cornflour
3 Tbsp caster sugar
600ml/1pt full-fat milk
2 egg yolks
Few drops vanilla extract
Few drops yellow food colouring (optional)

Makes approx. 600ml/1pt

In a saucepan, blend the cornflour with a little of the milk to make a smooth paste. Stir in the sugar and remaining milk. Heat, stirring, over the heat until boiling and thick – you may find it easier to use a whisk to help keep the mixture smooth.

Cook for 2 minutes. Remove from the heat and cool for 10 minutes. Stir in the egg yolks and return to the heat. Cook through for 3 minutes, stirring, but without boiling. Add vanilla extract to taste, and colour with food colouring if liked. To use cold, pour into a heatproof bowl and cover the surface with greaseproof paper to prevent a skin forming. Allow to cool before covering and chilling until required.

For a thicker pouring custard, use 1 Tbsp more cornflour.

Soups & Starters

Carrot and ginger soup

1 Tbsp butter

1 Tbsp olive oil

1 onion, chopped

2 cloves garlic, crushed

1 Tbsp very finely chopped
fresh ginger

2 tsp ground cumin

1 tsp curry powder

750g/1lb 10oz carrots,
chopped

1 large potato, diced

1 sweet potato, diced

1.5L/2¾pt chicken stock
(see page 18)

1 Tbsp runny honey

½ tsp salt

¼ tsp pepper

Serves 4

1. Melt the butter and oil in a large pan over medium heat. Add the onion, garlic and ginger and sauté over low heat until golden, for about 10 minutes. Add the cumin and curry powder and continue to sauté for a further minute. Add the vegetables and stock and simmer until the vegetables are tender, about 30 minutes.

2. Purée in batches until smooth and sieve back into the pot over low heat. Stir in the honey, salt and pepper. If liked, garnish with a mix of shredded mint (1 Tbsp) grated carrot (1 Tbsp), toasted sesame seeds (1 tsp) and honey (2 Tbsp).

Pea and mint soup

1kg/2lb 4oz frozen petits pois

1L/1¾pt chicken stock
 (see page 18)

10g/¼oz mint leaves,
 plus extra to garnish

100ml/3½fl oz double cream,
 plus extra to garnish

Salt and freshly ground black
 pepper

Serves 4

1. Put the peas and stock in a medium saucepan and bring to the boil. Turn off the heat, add the mint leaves, and leave to stand for 5 minutes. Transfer to a blender and liquidize until smooth. You may need to do this in two batches. If you prefer an extra-smooth soup then pass through a fine sieve. Return the soup to the pan and add the cream. Taste and season as required. Bring back to the boil before serving. Garnish with extra cream and mint leaves.

Tomato soup

2 Tbsp olive oil

2 large onions, finely
chopped

10 cloves garlic, roughly
chopped

2kg/4lb 8oz tomatoes, cut
into quarters

4 celery sticks, leaves
included, cut into 2.5cm/
1in pieces

6 whole cloves

6 sprigs parsley

1 large bunch basil, about
20g /¾oz

½–1 tsp white pepper

30g/1oz caster sugar
or to taste

Sea salt and freshly ground
black pepper to taste

To garnish:
Sprigs of parsley

Serves 4

1. Heat the oil in a large saucepan. Add the onions and
garlic and cook until they begin to sweat but do not allow
them to brown. Add the tomatoes, celery, cloves, parsley,
basil, white pepper and sugar. Bring to the boil, reduce
the heat and simmer until reduced to a pulp, about
40 minutes.

2. Pass the pulp through a mouli-légumes or fine sieve.
Return the tomato mixture to the pan and bring back to
the boil. Taste and add additional sugar, salt and pepper
if necessary. If the soup is too concentrated for your liking
dilute it by adding water to taste. Garnish with parsley.

Spring vegetable and pancetta soup

2 Tbsp olive oil

200g/7oz pancetta, cubed

1 onion, finely sliced

1 clove garlic, crushed

1 pinch chilli flakes

1.2L/2pt vegetable stock
(see page 19)

500g/1lb 2oz mashed
potato

150g/5½oz shelled peas

250g/9oz asparagus,
chopped into 2cm/¾in
pieces

150g/5½oz shelled
broad beans, or mange
touts, halved

200g/7oz mascarpone, half
in soup and half to garnish

10g/¼oz tarragon, shredded

Serves 4

1. Heat the oil in a large saucepan or stockpot. Add the pancetta and sauté until golden and cooked. Remove from the pan using a slotted spoon and drain on kitchen paper. Add the onion, garlic and chilli flakes to the pancetta oil and sauté for 3–4 minutes. Add the stock and mashed potato and bring to the boil. Add the peas, asparagus and broad beans and reduce the heat to a simmer. Continue to simmer for a further 6–8 minutes. Stir in the pancetta, mascarpone and tarragon and serve immediately, topped with an extra dollop of mascarpone.

Tuscan bean soup

400g/14oz dried
Tuscan beans (cannellini
and borlotti)

125ml/4fl oz olive oil

2 cloves garlic, finely
chopped

1 onion, diced

1 celery stick, diced

2 sprigs rosemary, needles
only, finely chopped

3 rashers streaky bacon,
diced

5 tsp tomato purée (paste)
or 420g/14oz tinned peeled
tomatoes

2 leeks, diced

2 courgettes (zucchini),
diced

1 bunch basil

2 sprigs parsley

salt and pepper

Serves 4

1. Soak the beans overnight in water. Drain and gently cook the beans in fresh water for about 2 hours, or until tender. Drain, reserving the liquid, and put about half the beans through a fine sieve or blender. Set aside.

2. Heat the oil in a large pan and gently sauté the garlic, onion, celery, rosemary and bacon until they begin to brown. Mix the tomato purée (paste) with a dash of warm water and stir into pan.

3. Add the, leeks, courgettes (zucchini), basil and parsley, as well as the puréed and whole beans, and their cooking water. Add a little extra hot water if necessary. This should be a thick soup so don't add too much. Season and taste, then cook for a further 30 minutes. Serve hot.

Butternut squash soup with blue cheese and walnuts

4 Tbsp butter

1 small onion, peeled and chopped

1 tsp salt + extra to taste

750g/1lb 10oz butternut squash, peeled and chopped into chunks

2 cloves

¼ tsp freshly grated nutmeg

Freshly ground black pepper to taste

750ml/1½pt vegetable stock

6 Tbsp toasted, chopped walnuts

6 Tbsp crumbled blue cheese

1 Tbsp chopped fresh flat leaf parsley

Serves 4

1. Heat 1 Tbsp of the butter in a large soup pot over medium heat. Add the onion and cook, stirring occasionally, until softened. Add the tsp of salt, squash, cloves and nutmeg and cook the mixture, covered, over a low heat for 10–15 minutes or until the squash is tender. Add the stock and simmer for a further 15 minutes.

2. Purée the soup (transfer to a food processor in stages or use a hand blender), then strain the soup back into the pot. Add salt and pepper to taste.

3. Heat the remaining butter in a frying pan until the butter is nut-brown. Add the toasted nuts and stir to coat.

4. Ladle the soup into four bowls and garnish with the browned butter, walnuts, blue cheese and parsley.

Smoked fish chowder

1L/1¾pt milk

4 sprigs parsley

1 tsp black peppercorns

2 dried chillies

600g/1lb 5oz fillets firm
  smoked fish e.g. cod,
  haddock or hake

100g/3½oz butter

1 onion, finely chopped

500g/1lb 2oz potatoes,
  chopped into 1cm/½in
  cubes

3 Tbsp plain flour

250ml/9fl oz white wine

Sea salt and freshly ground
  black pepper

3 Tbsp chopped parsley

Serves 4-6

1. Put the milk, parsley, peppercorns and chillies in a large heavy-based saucepan and bring to the boil. Reduce the heat to a simmer and add the fish fillets. Simmer for 3–4 minutes until the fish is cooked and flaky. Turn off the heat and remove the fish from the milk. Strain the milk and discard the black peppercorns, chilli and parsley.

2. Return the pan to the heat and add the butter. When the butter is sizzling, add the onion and potato and sauté for 3–4 minutes. Add the flour and stir to combine. Add the wine, stirring constantly, and allow to bubble. Still stirring, pour the milk into the pan and bring back to the boil. Reduce to a simmer and stir occasionally until thickened, about 6–8 minutes. Flake the fish and return to the pan, seasoning with salt and pepper to taste. Just before serving, stir in the chopped parsley and ladle into warmed bowls.

French onion soup

2 Tbsp olive oil

30g/1oz butter

850g/1lb 14oz (about 4) onions, thinly sliced

2 cloves garlic, crushed

1 tsp granulated sugar

1.2L/2pt beef stock (see page 18)

250ml/9fl oz dry white wine

Salt and freshly ground black pepper

2 Tbsp cognac (optional)

8–12 croûtons

200g/7oz Gruyère cheese, grated

Chopped parsley (optional)

Serves 4

1. Heat the oil and butter together in a large saucepan until very hot. Add the onions, garlic and sugar and stir for about 5 minutes until they start to darken on the edges. Reduce the heat to very low and leave to cook for a further 20–25 minutes, stirring very occasionally. The onions should caramelize and the base of the pan should have a dark caramelized film on it.

2. Add the stock and wine. Bring to the boil, scraping the film off the base of the pan. Reduce heat and simmer, uncovered, for about 50 minutes. Season to taste.

3. Bring the soup back to boiling point before serving and add the cognac if desired. Ladle the soup into heatproof bowls, top with croûtons and sprinkle with the Gruyére cheese. Place the bowls under the grill until the cheese is bubbling and golden. Sprinkle with chopped parsley if liked and serve immediately.

Sweet red pepper and oregano soup

2 onions, diced

50g/2oz butter

2 x 325g/11oz jars cooked
red peppers, drained

1 x 250g tin/8oz chopped
tomatoes

1 Tbsp demerara sugar

600ml/1pt strong chicken
stock

1 Tbsp Dijon mustard

salt and pepper

3 sprigs oregano, leaves only

Serves 6

1. Cook the onions in the butter very gently for at least 15 minutes – you want to cook them until they are very soft and sweet, almost caramelized. Add the red peppers, tinned tomatoes, sugar, stock and mustard. Simmer gently for 30 minutes.

2. Place the soup in the blender with the oregano reserve some for garnish) and blend until smooth. Season and taste. Serve garnished with oregano.

Chickpea and pimiento toasts

1 baguette

oil, for brushing

1 x 400g/14oz tin chickpeas

2 Tbsp olive oil

juice of 1 lemon

2 cloves garlic, crushed

2 Tbsp chopped fresh
parsley, plus extra for
garnish

2 tsp hot smoked paprika

4 pimientos de piquillo, cut
into strips

salt and freshly ground
black pepper

Makes 12

1. Slice the baguette into rounds about 1cm/½in thick and brush with a little oil. Place on a baking tray and bake in the oven for about 5 minutes or until golden brown.

2. Drain the chickpeas and rinse under cold water; set aside. Place the oil, lemon juice and crushed garlic in a bowl and whisk together. Stir in the chopped parsley and paprika and then add the drained chickpeas and pimiento strips. Stir vigorously, crushing the chickpeas lightly so that they hold together. Place a spoonful of chickpea mixture onto each toast and serve immediately, garnished with parsley.

Patatas bravas

1 medium onion, diced

1 Tbsp oil

½ bay leaf

1 guindilla chilli

1 tbsp plain flour

1 tsp hot smoked paprika, chilli powder or cayenne pepper

100ml/3½fl oz water

1.5kg/3¼lb Maris Piper potatoes, peeled

2 cloves garlic, crushed

salt

oil for frying

Serves 10

1. Heat the oil in frying pan. Add the onion and soften over a medium heat for a couple of minutes before adding the bay leaf and guindilla chilli. Cook for a further 2 or 3 minutes and then sprinkle on the flour and, stirring continuously, add the hot smoked paprika. Slowly add small amounts of the water, stirring continuously, until the sauce has the consistency of runny custard. Allow to simmer very gently for 10 minutes. Pass the sauce through a sieve and return to the heat.

2. If you are roasting the potatoes, preheat the oven to 230°C/450°F/Gas Mark 8. Cut the potatoes into small chunks and place in a lightly oiled roasting tin. Mix in the garlic, sprinkle with salt and roast for 20 minutes or until crisp and golden. To fry, cut the potatoes into thickish chips or ½cm/¼in slices and mix in the garlic. Season with salt. Heat the oil in a large frying pan and fry the potatoes gently until soft, increasing the heat at the end to turn them golden. Drain. Sprinkle the roasted or fried potatoes generously with the sauce and serve immediately.

Spanish omelette

3 large eggs
1 large clove garlic
750g/1lb 11oz Maris Piper
  potatoes, peeled and
  cubed
500g/1¼lb onions, diced
500ml/18fl oz oil for frying
salt

Makes 24 pieces

1. Break the eggs into a bowl and whisk. Finely grate the garlic into the eggs. Mix the potatoes and onions together in a bowl. Heat the oil in the frying pan, add the potato and onion mixture then turn down the heat slightly. Season with salt and stir the mixture repeatedly, so that it does not stick to the bottom, for 10 minutes or until the potato is cooked (test a piece with a fork). Turn the mixture out into a strainer over a bowl. (Reserve the oil for another dish.) After a minute, add the mixture to the eggs and stir thoroughly.

2. Return the pan to the heat and add just enough of the oil to cover the base in a thin film. After 30 seconds, add the egg and potato mixture, immediately spreading it evenly around the pan. Cook over a high heat, being extremely careful not to allow it to stick to the bottom. Remove from the heat.

3. After 2 minutes, oil a plate and place it over the frying pan, then carefully invert the pan (over the sink) to reveal a golden brown omelette. Return the pan to the heat, adding a teaspoon of the oil. After 10 seconds, slide the tortilla off the plate and into the pan. Cook for a further 1 minute. Turn out on to the plate. The golden brown tortilla should be set, yet still soft in the centre, the potatoes crumbly. Cut into eight segments, then cut each segment into three and serve.

Stuffed mussels

40 medium mussels in shells

2 medium onions, peeled
  and finely chopped

½ tsp salt

½ tsp caster sugar

100ml/3½fl oz olive oil

400ml/14fl oz hot water

1 lemon, peeled and sliced

For the stuffing:

130g/4½oz white rice

2 Tbsp currants

100ml/3½fl oz olive oil

100ml/3½fl oz sunflower oil

2 Tbsp pine kernels

6 medium onions, peeled
  and finely chopped

1 tsp cinnamon

1 tsp allspice

1 tsp white pepper

1 tsp salt

1 tsp sugar

100ml/3½fl oz hot water

½ bunch of fresh mint,
  chopped

Bunch of dill, chopped

Serves 10

1. Scrape the mussel shells with a knife or scrub with a brush. Soak in cold water while preparing the stuffing.

2. To make the stuffing, soak the rice in cold water for 30 minutes, then rinse thoroughly and drain. Soak the currants in warm water for about 15 minutes until they swell. Heat the olive and sunflower oils in a pan, add the pine kernels and onions, and brown slightly. Add the soaked rice and cook for 10 minutes. Then add the drained currants, spices, salt, sugar and hot water, and cook over a low heat for 15 minutes until the water has evaporated. Stir in the mint and dill, then set aside to cool.

3. Gently prise open each mussel with a knife without pulling the shells apart and remove the beard of the mussels, then rinse well and drain. Place a tablespoonful of rice stuffing into each shell and close tightly.

4. Add the onions into a large pan and place a sheet of damp greaseproof paper over them. Arrange the stuffed mussels on top in layers and add the salt, sugar, olive oil and hot water.

5. Arrange the lemon slices over the mussels and place another sheet of damp greaseproof paper on top, weighted down with a plate. Cover and bring to the boil over a high heat for approximately 40 minutes. When most of the liquid has evaporated and the mussels are opened, place in a serving dish with the onions and garnish with the lemon slices.

Prawn bruschetta with garlic

12 slices ciabatta

olive oil for drizzling

salt and pepper

225g/8oz cooked peeled
  prawns (shrimp), lightly
  chopped

2 eggs

2 Tbsp chopped garlic
  chives or 2 cloves garlic
  and 2 Tbsp chopped chives

2 Tbsp chopped flat-leaf
  parsley

4 Tbsp fresh breadcrumbs

grated rind and juice of
  2 lemons

Makes 12

1. Turn the grill on to full. Drizzle the ciabatta slices with oil
and sprinkle over a little salt and pepper then place on
the oven tray and grill (broil) on one side only. Set aside.

2. Mix all the remaining ingredients together, reserving
half the lemon juice and rind, until you have a thick,
gooey mixture that holds together.

3. Spread the mixture liberally on the untoasted side of
the ciabatta slices and grill (broil) until golden brown.
Serve immediately with a squeeze of lemon juice and a
sprinkling of grated lemon rind.

Roasted mixed peppers on toast

2 large red peppers

2 large yellow peppers

4 Tbsp olive oil

2 garlic cloves, peeled, one crushed, the other cut in half

2 Tbsp chopped parsley

Sea salt and freshly ground black pepper to taste

50g/2oz anchovy fillets, chopped or 2 Tbsp capers, rinsed

1 baguette, sliced diagonally

Serves 6

1. Preheat a barbecue, griddle pan or grill to a high heat. Grill the peppers whole until charred all over. Allow to cool. When cool enough to handle, peel the peppers, remove core and seeds and cut the flesh into thin strips.

2. Combine the olive oil, minced garlic, parsley, salt and pepper in a bowl. Add the pepper strips and stir to combine. Leave to marinate at room temperature for 1 hour, or in the refrigerator for up to one day. Bring to room temperature before serving.

3. Preheat the oven to 180ºC/350ºF/Gas mark 4. Slice the baguette into 3cm/1¼in thick slices. Arrange on a baking tray and toast for 2 minutes per side until slightly toasted. Rub the cut garlic over the toast. Top with the marinated pepper strips and serve.

Mozzarella and roasted red onion crostini

4 red onions, peeled and cut into wedges

olive oil for drizzling

2 Tbsp caster (superfine) sugar

6 slices country bread

salt and pepper

225g/8oz mozzarella, cut into bite-sized pieces

1 small bunch basil

Makes 12

1. Pre-heat the oven to 200°C/400°F/Gas mark 6.

2. Place the onions on a baking tray, drizzle with oil and sprinkle with the sugar. Cook until they become golden and soft. This will take about 30 minutes and can be done a day in advance.

3. Heat the griddle pan on the hob until smoking, drizzle the bread with oil and griddle the bread on both sides.

4. Slice the griddled bread in half, drizzle with oil and sprinkle over a little salt and pepper. Place the mozzarella and onions on the toasts, season, top with basil leaves and drizzle with oil.

Crab and chilli rissoles

1 Tbsp vegetable oil,
plus extra for frying

2 Tbsp desiccated coconut

2 tsp tamarind purée (see
page 19)

200g/7oz finely chopped
onion

350g/12oz fresh white crab
meat

150g/5oz fresh brown crab
meat

1 Tbsp tomato purée

2 or 3 green chillies, chopped

salt, to taste

1 Tbsp chopped fresh
coriander leaves, to garnish

Masala:

10–12 fresh or dried curry
leaves (optional)

2 tsp ground coriander

1 tsp turmeric

½ tsp chilli powder

½ tsp black/brown mustard
seeds

Serves 4

1. Heat the oil in a karahi or wok. Add the masala and stir-fry for 30 seconds. Add the coconut and stir-fry for 1 minute then add the tamarind and onion and continue stir-frying for 5 more minutes.

2. Add the crab meat, tomato purée and green chillies and turn off the heat. Season with salt.

3. Using your hands, form the mixture into rounds about 5–6 cm/2–2½ inches in diameter.

4. Heat the oil for frying in a frying pan. Add the rissoles and fry for about 1 minute on each side until brown. Serve garnished with coriander leaves.

Mushroom crostini

4 Tbsp olive oil

1 fat clove garlic, peeled and crushed

1 small thin French baguette, cut into 12 slices

250g/9oz chestnut mushrooms, chopped

2 Tbsp freshly chopped parsley

Salt and freshly ground black pepper

40g/1½ oz Parmesan, shaved

Serves 4

1. Preheat the oven to 200°C/400°F/Gas Mark 6. Drizzle 3 Tbsp of the olive oil on a baking tray, add the garlic and then, using your hands, spread the oil and garlic all over the tray. Add the slices of bread, rubbing and turning them until they are coated with the garlicky oil.

2. Bake for 10–15 minutes until golden. Keep an eye on them to prevent them from becoming too brown.

3. Heat the remaining oil in a frying pan and cook the mushrooms for 8–10 minutes. Stir in the parsley and seasoning then top each slice of bread with the mushroom mixture. Sprinkle with shaved parmesan and serve immediately before the bread starts to go soft.

Parmesan-coated chicken goujons with pesto dip

For the pesto dip:

1 bunch basil, leaves only

50g/2oz pine nuts

2 Tbsp grated Parmesan

225ml/8fl oz extra-virgin olive oil

2 cloves garlic

salt and pepper

For the goujons:

2 large chicken breasts, skinless and boneless

125g/4oz plain flour, seasoned with salt and pepper

2 eggs, beaten

50g/2oz Parmesan and 50g/2oz matzo meal, mixed together in a bowl oil for frying

1 lemon for squeezing

Makes 12 goujons

1. First make the pesto. Place the basil, pine nuts, 2 tbsp of the Parmesan, olive oil, garlic and seasoning in the processor and blend until just smooth. Check the taste, season and set aside.

2. Cut the chicken breasts into strips – you should get about six out of each breast. Put the seasoned flour, beaten egg and the Parmesan and matzo mixture in three separate bowls. Dip the chicken strips one by one into the flour to coat all over, then place in the egg, coating all over, and finally roll them in the Parmesan and matzo mixture. Chill the coated strips in the fridge for 30 minutes.

3. Heat the oil until it sizzles when a crumb is put into it. Carefully fry each chicken strip – if the outside is getting rather dark take the chicken out and place in a pre-heated oven (180°C/350°F/Gas mark 4) for 5 minutes. This is to ensure that the chicken is cooked through. Once all the chicken goujons are thoroughly cooked squeeze the lemon over them and serve with the pesto on the side for dipping.

Samosas

2 Tbsp vegetable oil,
  plus extra for deep-frying
450g/1lb strong white plain
  flour, plus a little
extra for pastry-making
sweet and sour brown
  tamarind chutney (see
  page 22), to serve

Vegetable filling:
2 large potatoes, peeled,
  cooked and lightly mashed
½ cup fresh peas, cooked or
  frozen peas, thawed
1 tsp salt
1 tsp garam masala
1 tsp ground black pepper
¼ tsp chilli powder
1 tsp ground coriander
1 tsp ground cumin
chopped fresh coriander
1 tsp dried fenugreek
  leaves (optional)
1–3 green chillies, finely
  chopped (optional)

Makes 16

1. Mix the ingredients for the samosa filling together in a bowl and set aside.

2. For the samosa pastry, mix together the measured oil, flour and enough water to make a dough which, when mixed, does not stick to the bowl. Leave it to stand for about 1 hour. Divide the dough into 4, then shape each piece into a square. Roll out each square on a floured surface and cut each into 4 rectangles measuring 7.5 x 20 cm/3 x 8 inches. Remember, the thinner you roll the pastry, the crisper the samosas will be.

3. Take one pastry rectangle and place a teaspoon of filling at one end. Make the first diagonal fold, then the second and third. Open the pouch and top up with some more filling but do not overfill or the samosa will burst during deep-frying. Brush some flour and water on the remaining flap, and seal. Trim off the excess pastry. Make the remaining samosas in the same way.

4. Heat the oil in a deep frying pan to 190°C/375°F (chip-frying temperature). Add one samosa to the hot oil. After a few seconds add the next, and continue until the surface area of the pan is full but not crowded. This maintains the oil temperature. Fry for 8–10 minutes.

5. Remove the samosas from the pan using a slotted spoon. Shake off the excess oil and drain them on absorbent kitchen paper. Repeat until all the samosas are cooked then serve them hot with the chutney.

Tomato fritters

Savoury choux pastry:

125ml/4fl oz water

50g/2oz unsalted butter

salt and pepper

75g/2¾oz plain flour

2 eggs

100g/4oz grated Parmesan cheese

18 cherry tomatoes or baby plum tomatoes

100g/3½ oz mozzarella, chopped into small cubes

1 small bunch basil, leaves torn into small pieces

2 fresh white anchovy fillets, finely chopped

salt and pepper

vegetable oil for frying

Serves 6

1. First make the choux pastry. Pour the water into a saucepan. Add the butter, salt and pepper and bring the mixture to the boil. Take the pan off the heat and gently tip in all the flour all in one go. Stirring constantly, heat again and cook until the mixture turns into a smooth, glossy paste and comes away from the side of the pan. Take the pan off the heat and leave to cool. Beat the eggs into the mixture one at a time. Stir in the grated Parmesan cheese at the end.

2. Slice off the top of the tomatoes (the end where the stalk is), scoop out the pulp and place upside down to drain out any juice.

3. In a bowl mix the mozzarella, basil and anchovies together then season with salt and pepper. Fill the tomatoes with the cheese mixture.

4. Take a small amount of the choux mixture (about the size of a ping pong ball) and make a flat pattie in your hand. Place the tomato in the middle and wrap the choux mixture around it so the tomato is totally covered. Roll it in your hand.

5. Heat the oil until slightly smoking. Drop the fritters into the hot oil until they puff up and go golden brown. Take out of the oil with a slotted spoon and drain on absorbent kitchen paper. Serve immediately, garnished with fresh basil.

Pork brochettes

900g/2lb loin of pork,
  cut into 2cm/¾in cubes

50ml/2fl oz white wine

50ml/2fl oz light olive oil

3 large cloves garlic,
  crushed

2 tsp hot smoked paprika,
  chilli powder or cayenne
  pepper (or 1 tsp of hot
  smoked paprika, chilli
  powder or cayenne pepper
  and 1 tsp mild smoked
  paprika, if you prefer)

½ bay leaf, crumbled

2 tsp chopped fresh thyme

salt and freshly ground black
  pepper

2 lemons, quartered
  (optional)

Makes about 20

1. Arrange the meat in a wide, shallow, non-metallic dish. Mix together all the other ingredients, except the lemons, and season. Pour the mixture over the meat, cover and leave to marinate, preferably in the fridge, for at least 8 hours, turning once or twice. Thread three cubes onto each skewer and cook on a very hot griddle or grill, turning once or twice, for about 8 minutes. The meat will be charred slightly, but still juicy. Squeeze over the juice of the lemon wedges, if you wish, and serve hot.

Coriander chicken on lemongrass skewers

4 skinless, boneless chicken breasts

1 small bunch coriander

2 red chillies, diced

4 kaffir lime leaves, thinly sliced

12 lemongrass stalks

2 Tbsp fish sauce

2 Tbsp dried Japanese breadcrumbs

oil for deep-frying

sweet chilli sauce, to serve

Makes 20

1. Place the chicken, coriander, chillies, kaffir lime leaves, 2 of the lemongrass stalks and fish sauce in the food processor. Process until smooth.

2. Put the chicken mixture in a bowl and mix in the breadcrumbs very thoroughly. They will bind the mixture together.

3. Prepare the lemon grass skewers by peeling off the outer layer of the remaining 10 lemon grass stalks. Trim both ends at an angle so you almost get a sharp point and then cut each stalk in half.

4. Heat the oil for deep-frying in the frying pan. Take a generous teaspoon of the chicken mixture and mould into a ball using your hand. Carefully put it into the oil. Fry gently for 5 minutes.

5. Drain on absorbent kitchen paper and then skewer each ball on to a lemongrass stalk. Serve with a sweet chilli dipping sauce. The chicken mixture can be made up to two days in advance. The chicken balls can be fried 3 hours before serving and then heated in the oven just before serving.

Prawn croquettes

100g/3½ oz butter

125g/4oz plain flour

750ml/1¼ pt cold milk

salt and pepper

400g/14oz cooked peeled
  prawns, diced

2 tsp tomato purée

5 or 6 Tbsp fine breadcrumbs

2 large eggs, beaten

oil for deep-frying

Makes about 36

1. Melt the butter in a medium saucepan and add the flour, stirring continuously. Allow the flour to cook in the butter for a couple of minutes, continuing to stir. Start adding the cold milk little by little, stirring all the while until you have a thick, smooth sauce. Add the prawns, season well and stir in the tomato paste. Continue to cook for 7 or 8 minutes. The end result should be quite thick. It is essential that the mixture is allowed to cool completely – overnight is best.

2. Take a scant tablespoon of the mixture and form into a croqueta, a 3-4 cm/1½–2 in cylinder. Roll the croqueta in the breadcrumbs, then coat in the beaten egg, then roll in the breadcrumbs again. Make sure the breadcrumbs are always dry to ensure an even coating.

3. Heat the oil for deep-frying in a large, heavy-based pan until the temperature reaches 180°C/350°F or a cube of bread turns golden brown in 20–30 seconds. Fry in batches of no more than 3 or 4 for about 5 minutes until golden brown. Remove with a slatted spoon, drain on absorbent kitchen paper and serve immediately.

Chickpea and sweetcorn cheese cakes

90g/3oz chickpea, gram or besan flour

60g/2oz fine cornmeal

2 tsp baking powder

½ tsp salt

1 tsp caster sugar

30g/1oz finely grated fresh Parmesan cheese

1 egg, separated

60g/2oz sweetcorn kernels

250ml/8fl oz milk

60g/2oz butter, melted

1 Tbsp vegetable oil

Smoked paprika

Makes 8

1. Sift the flour, cornmeal, baking powder, salt and sugar into a bowl. Stir in the grated cheese. Make a well in the centre and add the egg yolk, sweetcorn, milk and melted butter. Whisk into the dry ingredients to form a thick, smooth batter. Take care not to over-beat. Whisk the egg white until stiff then carefully fold into the batter.

2. Heat a large frying pan or griddle until hot. Brush with a little oil and pour about 90ml/3fl oz of batter into the centre of the pan. Cook over low to moderate heat for about 2 minutes on each side, until golden. Alternatively, cook in a crêpe pan – about 15cm/6in diameter base.

3. Turn the griddle cake out onto a wire rack lined with a clean tea towel and baking parchment. Cover the cake to keep moist. Make 8 griddle cakes in total, re-oiling the pan as necessary and stacking the cooked griddle cakes between sheets of parchment, until you are ready to serve. Best served warm, buttered and sprinkled with smoked paprika.

Chickpeas and tahini dip

420g/15oz tinned cooked
  chickpeas

1 garlic clove, peeled and
  crushed

180ml/6fl oz water

4 Tbsp tahini

125ml/4fl oz lemon juice

Pinch of salt

Parsley sprigs,

½ tsp paprika and 2 Tbsp
  olive oil, to garnish

Serves 4

1. Reserve 1 teaspoon of chickpeas for the garnish. Using a food processor or blender, process or blend until smooth the remaining chickpeas with the garlic and 60ml/2fl oz of the water.

2. Dissolve the tahini in the remaining water and lemon juice, then blend with the chickpea mixture. The mixture should be thick and smooth. Season with salt.

3. Pour the mixture into small dishes and garnish with the reserved chickpeas, parsley sprigs, paprika and olive oil. Serve with pitta bread and/or barbecued meat or chicken.

Meat

Very quick chicken curry

4 skinless, boneless chicken breasts, cut into strips

Juice of 1 lemon

4 Tbsp tikka or mild curry paste

2 Tbsp groundnut oil

1 mango, peeled and sliced

2 garlic cloves, crushed

150g/5oz Greek yoghurt

55g/2oz flaked almonds, toasted

4 Tbsp coriander, roughly chopped

To serve:
Basmati rice

Serves 3–4

1. Put the chicken strips in a large bowl and sprinkle with lemon juice. Add the tikka or curry paste. Mix well. Set aside to marinate for 10 minutes.

2. Heat a large work or frying pan and add 1 Tbsp oil. Add the chicken with its marinade and cook for 5–7 minutes until the chicken is golden and cooked. Remove and set aside.

3. Bring the wok back up to heat. Add the remaining oil and add the mango and garlic and stir-fry for a further 1 minute. Return the chicken to the pan and stir-fry until the chicken is heated through. Stir in the yogurt. Sprinkle over the toasted almonds and coriander and serve with basmati rice.

Kung Po chicken

4 boneless, skinless chicken breasts, cut into small chunks

4 tsp grated root ginger or ginger purée

2 Tbsp light soy sauce

2 tsp cornflour

8 spring onions

4 Tbsp groundnut oil

200g/8oz unsalted, unroasted peanuts

6 dried red chillies, deseeded and chopped

1 tsp caster sugar

4 tsp rice vinegar

Serves 4

1. Put the chicken in a bowl. Whisk together the ginger, soy sauce and cornflour until smooth, pour over the chicken and stir until evenly coated. Set aside in fridge to marinate for at least 1 hour.

2. Trim the spring onions. Remove the green tops from two of them and chop finely. Slice the rest of these two onions, and the other two whole ones, into 2.5cm/1in lengths.

3. Heat the oil in a wok and stir-fry the peanuts over a high heat for 1 minute or until golden. Drain the nuts from the wok with a slotted spoon and set aside.

4. Lower the heat to medium-high, add the chicken with its marinade and sliced spring onions and stir-fry for 3 minutes. Add the nuts and chillies, sprinkle over the sugar and rice vinegar and toss together over the heat for 2 minutes.

5. Sprinkle over the chopped spring onion tops and serve at once with rice or egg noodles.

Red pesto chicken with olives

2 tbsp olive oil

4 boneless, skinless chicken breasts

½ red pepper, deseeded and chopped

½ yellow or orange pepper, deseeded and chopped

1 courgette, sliced or cut into julienne

2 garlic cloves, peeled and crushed

100ml/3½fl oz dry white wine

150ml/¼pt chicken stock

3 Tbsp sun-dried tomato purée

2 Tbsp red pesto

4 Tbsp crème fraîche or double cream

Salt and freshly ground black pepper

12 black olives

Handful of fresh basil leaves

Serves 4

1. Heat the olive oil in a wok and brown the chicken breasts, two at a time, on both sides over a fairly high heat. Remove them from the wok and set aside.

2. Add the peppers, courgette and garlic to the wok and stir-fry for 5 minutes until starting to soften. Pour in the wine and let it bubble for 1 minute, then stir in the stock, tomato purée and red pesto.

3. Return the chicken to the wok, lower the heat, cover and simmer for 15 minutes or until the breasts are cooked through.

4. Stir in the crème fraîche or double cream and season to taste. Serve with the olives and basil leaves scattered over.

Lemon chicken stir-fry with cashew nuts

For the sauce:

150ml/5fl oz fresh chicken
  stock

1 tsp cornflour

1 Tbsp runny honey

2 Tbsp soy sauce

2 Tbsp groundnut oil

340g/12oz chicken fillets,
  cut into strips

2 garlic cloves, finely sliced

2 large courgettes, thinly
  sliced

Grated rind of ½ lemon and
  juice of 1 lemon

55g/2oz unsalted
  cashew nuts

To serve:

Steamed brown rice

Serves 3

1. To make the sauce, mix the stock, cornflour, honey and soy sauce in a small bowl and set aside.

2. Heat the oil in a large frying pan or wok. Add the chicken and stir-fry for 3–4 minutes until golden. Add the garlic and cook for a further minute. Remove from the pan and set aside.

3. Re-heat the pan and add 4 Tbsp water. When the water is boiling add the courgettes and stir-fry for 2 minutes. Return the chicken to the pan with the sauce and cook for a further 2 minutes until the sauce has reduced.

4. Add the lemon rind, juice and cashew nuts, stir through until well combined and serve with steamed brown rice.

Chicken biryani

Medium whole chicken, cut
into 8 pieces

2L/70fl oz water

2 dried limes or the rind of
1 orange

2 chicken stock cubes

500g/1lb 2oz basmati rice,
rinsed and drained

2 Tbsp butter

3 medium onions, peeled
and sliced

250g/9oz yogurt

1 tsp cornflour ¾ tsp of each:
black pepper, cumin,
fresh coriander, turmeric,
cardamom and cinnamon

3 garlic cloves, peeled and
crushed

1 tsp ground saffron, soaked
in 60ml/2fl oz hot water

Fried whole almonds, pine
nuts and pistachio nuts, to
garnish

Serves 4–6

1. Place the chicken pieces and water in a large
saucepan. Bring to the boil, skimming whenever
necessary. Add the dried limes or orange rind and the
chicken stock cubes. Cover and simmer over a low heat
for 30 to 40 minutes until tender. Remove the chicken
from the stock and set aside. Add the rice to the stock in
the pan and cook for 10 minutes until the rice is almost
cooked. Drain and set aside.

2. Heat the butter in a large saucepan and fry the
onions for 5 to 7 minutes, until golden brown. Stir in
the cooked chicken.

3. In a bowl, mix the yoghurt with the cornflour. Strain
through a sieve into a heavy-based saucepan. Place
the pan over a medium heat, stirring constantly in one
direction with a wooden spoon until the yoghurt starts to
boil. Reduce the heat and simmer gently, uncovered, for
3 minutes, stirring occasionally.

4. Add all the spices and garlic to the pan. Pour the
boiled yoghurt over the chicken. Add half the cooked
rice to cover the chicken, then sprinkle with half the
saffron water. Add the remaining rice and saffron water.
Cover and simmer for 25 to 30 minutes until the rice is
tender. Transfer to a large dish and garnish with fried
almonds, pine nuts and pistachios.

Baked chicken legs

8 chicken drumsticks, skinned

For the Marinade:
about 120ml/4fl oz milk
200g/7oz plain yogurt
200ml/7fl oz single cream
2 Tbsp vegetable oil
2 Tbsp fresh lemon juice
3 or 4 cloves garlic, chopped
2.5cm/1in piece of fresh root ginger, chopped
2 or 3 fresh red chillies, chopped
1 Tbsp finely chopped fresh coriander
2 Tbsp ground almonds
1 tsp salt

For the Masala:
2 Tbsp ground coriander
1 Tbsp garam masala
2 tsp cardamom pods, ground
1 tsp fennel seeds

Serves 4

1. Adding the milk little by little, put all the marinade ingredients and the masala in a blender or food processor and 'pulse' to a pourable purée.

2. Cut small gashes in the chicken drumsticks using a sharp knife and work the marinade into the flesh. Put the drumsticks in a shallow non-aluminium bowl with all the excess marinade. Cover and refrigerate for up to 24 hours.

3. To cook, put the chicken drumsticks, topped by any excess marinade in an oven tray. Cover with foil and cook in a preheated oven, 190°C/375°F/Gas Mark 5, for 10 minutes.

4. Turn the drumsticks over, baste with the marinade, cover again with foil and cook for 10 minutes more.

5 Using a sharp knife, cut to the bone to test that the chicken is fully cooked – the juices should run clear.

6. There will be a reasonable amount of cooked marinade in the oven tray. Place this in a saucepan and mix well. When simmering, pour it over the drumsticks to serve.

Pad Thai with shredded omelette

350g/12oz dried medium flat rice stick noodles

2 Tbsp vegetable oil

4 large eggs

4 shallots, peeled and sliced

1 boneless, skinless chicken breast, cut into small chunks

200g/7oz raw tiger prawns, peeled

1 Tbsp oyster sauce

2 Tbsp Thai fish sauce

Juice of 1 lime

1 tsp brown sugar

225g/8oz beansprouts

4 spring onions, shredded

100g/4oz natural roasted peanuts, roughly chopped

1 red chilli, deseeded and finely chopped

2 Tbsp chopped fresh coriander

Serves 4

1. Cook the rice noodles according to the packet instructions, then drain and set aside.

2. Heat 1 tablespoon of the oil in a wok. Beat one of the eggs and pour into the wok, tilting the pan so the egg spreads out in a very thin layer. Cook until the underneath has set, then flip it over to cook the other side. Slide the omelette out of the pan on to a plate and keep warm in a low oven.

3. Add the rest of the oil to the wok and stir-fry the shallots and chicken over a fairly high heat for 2 minutes. Add the prawns and stir-fry for 1 minute.

4. Beat the remaining eggs, pour into the pan and stir until the eggs scramble. Add the oyster sauce, fish sauce, lime juice, sugar and noodles and stir-fry for 2 minutes.

5. Add the bean sprouts, spring onions and half the peanuts and toss everything together over the heat until piping hot.

6. Transfer to serving plates and scatter over the remaining peanuts. Roll up the omelette, slice thinly and scatter over the noodles with the chilli and coriander.

Chicken wings with coriander

24 chicken wings

400ml/14fl oz vegetable oil

4 garlic cloves, peeled and crushed

Bunch of coriander, finely chopped

1 Tbsp pomegranate paste

100ml/3½fl oz lemon juice

Pinch of salt and freshly ground black pepper

For the garnish:

Lettuce leaves

Fresh coriander leaves

Lemon wedges

Serves 4

1. Rinse the chicken wings in cold water and drain. Heat the oil in a pan and fry the wings in batches until golden brown and almost tender.

2. Mix in the garlic, coriander, pomegranate paste and lemon juice. Season with salt and pepper.

3. Transfer the chicken wings to a serving dish and drizzle with the cooking juice. Garnish with lettuce leaves, fresh coriander and lemon wedges.

Turkey burgers with cranberry relish

500g/1lb turkey mince

250g/8oz pork mince

1 small onion, peeled and finely chopped

1 Tbsp wholegrain mustard

2 Tbsp tomato ketchup

1 small bunch thyme

4 Tbsp dry white breadcrumbs

Salt and freshly ground black pepper

2 Tbsp sunflower oil

For the relish:

1 small red onion, peeled and thinly sliced

125g/4oz cranberries

100ml/3½fl oz cloudy apple juice

1 eating apple, washed, cored and chopped

1 medium orange, peeled, segmented and chopped

2 Tbsp maple syrup

Serves 4

1. First make the burgers. Place the turkey mince and pork mince in a bowl and mix in the onion. Add the mustard and ketchup. Strip the leaves from the thyme and add them to the mixture together with the breadcrumbs and seasoning. Bring together with your hands.

2. Divide into eight equal pieces and form each into a rough burger shape about 1cm/½in thick. Place on a plate lined with baking parchment and chill for 30 minutes.

3. Meanwhile, make the relish. Place the onion and cranberries in a saucepan and pour over the apple juice. Bring to the boil, cover and simmer for about 5 minutes until the cranberries are just softened. Remove from the heat and allow to cool.

4. When you are ready to cook the burgers, heat the oil in a large frying pan and gently fry the burgers for 10–12 minutes on each side until golden and cooked through. Drain on absorbent kitchen paper and keep warm.

5. To finish the relish, gently mix the chopped apple into the cranberries together with the chopped orange segments and maple syrup. Pile into a serving bowl and serve with the burgers.

Turkey meatballs in a rich tomato sauce

450g/1lb turkey mince

1 Tbsp fresh thyme leaves

2 garlic cloves, peeled and crushed

2 tsp Dijon mustard

50g/2oz fresh breadcrumbs

1 egg, beaten

2 Tbsp sunflower oil

2 rashers of back bacon, chopped

½ red pepper, deseeded and chopped

2 x 400g/14oz tins chopped tomatoes

2 Tbsp tomato purée

150ml/¼pt red wine or chicken stock

Salt and freshly ground black pepper

Serves 4

1. In a large bowl, mix together the turkey mince, half the thyme, garlic, mustard and breadcrumbs. Stir in the beaten egg and, with damp hands, roll the mixture into about 24 walnut-sized balls.

2. Place the meatballs on a plate in a single layer, cover with cling film and chill in the fridge for 1 hour or longer.

3. Heat the oil in a wok, add half the meatballs and fry over a medium heat until evenly browned all over. Lift out of the wok with a draining spoon and fry the rest of the meatballs in the same way.

4. Add the bacon to the wok and fry until lightly browned. Add the red pepper, tomatoes, tomato purée and wine or stock and season to taste. Return the meatballs to the wok, lower the heat, cover and simmer for 20 minutes. Serve with the rest of the thyme sprinkled over.

Spicy beef stir-fry

2 Tbsp soy sauce

1 Tbsp sesame oil

1 tsp cornflour

450g/1lb sirloin or fillet steak, thinly sliced

2 Tbsp groundnut oil

1 mild red chilli, finely diced

2 garlic cloves, finely chopped

2 Tbsp fresh ginger, finely chopped

225g/8oz fine green beans

225g/8oz brown-capped mushrooms, sliced

1 red pepper, finely sliced

2 small heads pak choy, leaves separated from stem

Serves 4

1. In a small bowl, combine the soy sauce, sesame oil and cornflour, and marinate the steak for 10 minutes.

2. Heat a large wok or frying pan and add 1 Tbsp oil. Add the chilli, garlic and ginger and stir-fry for 30 seconds. Add the beans, mushrooms and red pepper and stir-fry for a further 3–5 minutes until tender. Remove the vegetables and wipe the pan clean.

3. Re-heat the pan and add the remaining groundnut oil. Stir-fry the beef strips in batches, for 2 minutes per batch. Remove and keep warm. Return the beef and vegetables to the pan. Add the pak choy and heat through. Serve with fried rice.

Moussaka

4 Tbsp olive oil

1kg/2lb 3 oz minced meat

2 onions, peeled and finely
chopped

125ml/4fl oz white wine

4 tomatoes, pulped

Salt and freshly ground
black pepper

3 medium eggs, beaten

110g/4oz feta cheese,
crumbled

110g/4oz breadcrumbs

1kg/2lb 3oz aubergines,
cubed

1kg/2lb 3oz courgettes,
cubed

2 Tbsp butter, for greasing

For the béchamel sauce:

4 Tbsp butter

8 Tbsp plain flour

2L/4½fl oz milk

30g/1oz Parmesan cheese,
grated

2 eggs, yolks beaten

Pinch of salt, freshly ground
black pepper and nutmeg

Serves 6

1. Heat the olive oil in a pan and fry the minced meat
and onions until lightly browned. Pour in the wine, add the
tomatoes, season with salt and pepper and cook for
30 minutes, stirring regularly. Then stir in the eggs, feta
cheese and breadcrumbs.

2. In a separate pan, fry the aubergines and courgettes
until lightly cooked.

3. Grease a 25 cm/10 in square baking pan with the
butter and alternate a layer of vegetables with a layer of
meat. Repeat until the mixtures are finished. Preheat the
oven to 190°C/375°F/Gas Mark 5.

4. To make the sauce, melt the butter in a pan. Remove
from the heat and stir in the flour. Return to the heat,
gradually adding in the milk and stirring all the while,
and simmer for 9 minutes until thick. Add the Parmesan
cheese and egg yolks. Stir until thick, then remove from
the heat and season.

5. Pour the sauce over the meat and vegetable mixtures
and bake for 1 hour until golden.

Stuffed vegetables

For the vegetables:

5 red peppers

5 green peppers

15 small aubergines

15 small courgettes

6 small potatoes

500g/1lb 2oz vine leaves

500ml/17fl oz hot water

750ml/1½ pt chicken stock

2 Tbsp lemon juice

For the stuffing:

1.5kg/3lb 5oz minced
  beef or lamb

800g/1lb 12oz short
  grain rice

90g/3oz parsley,
  chopped

90g/3oz fresh coriander,
  chopped

2 medium tomatoes, diced

2 medium onions, finely
  chopped

3 garlic cloves, peeled and
  crushed

100g/3½oz butter

½ tsp of each: black pepper,
  cumin and allspice

1 Tbsp salt

Serves 8–10

1. Thoroughly rinse all the vegetables. Cut the tops off the peppers and remove the seeds and white membrane, then rinse and drain. Cut the tops off the potatoes. Cut the stems and tops off the aubergines and courgettes. Scoop out the flesh of the potatoes, aubergines and courgettes using a special scooping tool or a spoon, leaving 5mm/¼in of the flesh. Be careful not to break the shells while scooping. Rinse and drain. Soak the vine leaves in the hot water for 10 minutes. Drain and remove the stems.

2. To make the stuffing, thoroughly combine all the ingredients in a large bowl. Fill the peppers, aubergines, courgettes and potato shells with the stuffing. Do not fill the vegetables completely as there should be enough space for the rice to expand. Place an amount of stuffing the size of a small finger in the middle of a vine leaf on the stem side. Fold the sides of the vine leaf over the stuffing, then roll it up firmly but not too tightly. Repeat until all the stuffing is finished. Neatly arrange the stuffed vine leaves in a large dish.

3. Place any unused vine leaves in the bottom of a large heavy-based saucepan. Arrange the stuffed potatoes and peppers in an upright position in the pan. Place the aubergines and courgettes horizontally on top of the potatoes and peppers and arrange the stuffed vine leaves on top. Pour 125ml/4fl oz of the chicken stock, the lemon juice and water over, to cover. Cover with a plate to keep them in place. Bring to the boil, then reduce the heat. Simmer gently until most of the liquid has been absorbed. Gradually add the remaining chicken stock and simmer gently for 1½ hours. Carefully remove the dolmas from the pan and arrange them in a serving dish.

Five spice steak with peppers

2 Tbsp vegetable oil

500g/1lb 2oz rump steak,
  cut into thin strips

1 red onion, peeled and
  thinly sliced

1 onion, peeled and thinly
  sliced

1 red pepper, deseeded and
  thinly sliced

1 green pepper, deseeded
  and thinly sliced

1 yellow pepper, deseeded
  and thinly sliced

2 garlic cloves, peeled and
  finely chopped

1 tsp Chinese five-spice
  powder

150ml/¼pt beef stock

1 tsp cornflour

2 Tbsp dark soy sauce

Serves 4

1. Heat half the oil in a wok and stir-fry the steak in
two batches over a high heat for 3–4 minutes or until
browned. Remove from the wok and set aside.

2. Lower the heat to medium-high, add the rest of the oil
and stir-fry the onions for 3 minutes. Add the peppers
and the garlic and stir-fry for 3 minutes.

3. Return the steak to the wok, sprinkle in the five spice
powder and stir-fry for 1 minute. Mix the stock and
cornflour together until smooth, pour into the wok and
add the soy sauce. Stir-fry for 1 minute until the sauce
bubbles and coats the meat and vegetables.
Serve immediately.

Chilli bean beef with nachos and cheese

2 Tbsp sunflower oil

1 onion, peeled and chopped

500g/1lb 2oz lean minced steak

2 tsp hot chilli powder

300ml/½pt beef stock

400g/14oz tin chopped tomatoes

2 Tbsp sun-dried tomato purée

400g/14oz tin red kidney beans, drained and rinsed

To serve:

Large bag nachos

100g/4oz grated mature Cheddar cheese

1 avocado, stoned, peeled and chopped

Soured cream

Serves 4

1. Heat the oil in a wok and fry the onion over a low heat until soft. Increase the heat to medium-high, add the minced steak, breaking up any clumps of meat with a wooden spoon, and fry until browned.

2. Add the chilli powder, fry for 1 minute and then add the stock, tomatoes and tomato purée. Simmer for 30 minutes.

3. Stir in the kidney beans and simmer for a further 10 minutes or until most of the liquid has evaporated and the sauce is thick and not too wet.

4. Meanwhile, spread out the nachos on a foil-lined grill rack and sprinkle with the cheese. Grill until the cheese melts.

5. Spoon the mince and beans into a serving dish and surround with the cheesy nachos and avocado. Serve with the soured cream to spoon over.

Marinated steak in tomato and wild mushroom sauce

4 sirloin or rump steaks

2 garlic cloves, peeled and finely chopped

150ml/¼pt red wine

6 Tbsp olive oil

Juice of ½ lemon

Freshly ground black pepper

1 large onion, peeled and finely chopped

150g/5oz mixed mushrooms, chopped

500g/1lb 2oz ripe tomatoes, skinned, deseeded and chopped

2 Tbsp chopped fresh parsley

Serves 4

1. Lay the steaks in a shallow dish in a single layer. Mix together the garlic, red wine, 2 tablespoons of the olive oil and the lemon juice and season with plenty of freshly ground black pepper. Pour over the steaks, cover with clingfilm and leave in the fridge to marinate for several hours or overnight.

2. Put 2 tablespoons of the olive oil in a wok and, over a low heat, sauté the onion and mushrooms for 5 minutes. Lift the steaks from the marinade and set aside. Add the marinade to the wok with the tomatoes and simmer for 25–30 minutes until excess liquid has evaporated and the sauce is thick. Pour the sauce into a heatproof dish and keep warm in a low oven.

3. Carefully rinse the wok and wipe clean with absorbent kitchen paper. Heat the rest of the oil in the wok and fry the steaks over a high heat until browned on both sides. Lower the heat and continue to cook until done to your liking.

4. Serve the steaks with the sauce spooned over, sprinkled with chopped parsley.

Spaghetti bolognaise

1 Tbsp olive oil

500g/1lb mince (beef or lamb)

1 large onion, peeled and chopped

1 stick celery, chopped

3 cloves garlic, chopped or crushed

1 small carrot, peeled and chopped

3 Tbsp chopped leek

1 tsp dried mixed herbs or oregano

1 tsp fresh chopped thyme

1 stock cube (chicken or vegetable)

2 tsp tomato purée

2 x 400g/14oz tins chopped tomatoes

Salt and pepper

300g/11oz spaghetti (or other pasta shapes)

Grated Parmesan cheese or Cheddar cheese (optional), to serve

Serves 4

1. Heat 1 tbsp olive oil in a large saucepan over a medium heat. Add the mince to the pan and cook for 3-4 minutes or until browned stirring occasionally and breaking down the mince with a wooden spoon.

2. Add the chopped onion, celery, garlic, carrot and leek to the pan along with the dried herbs and thyme. Crumble the stock cube into the pan and stir well. Cook for a further 2–3 minutes.

3. Add the tomato purée and cook for 1 minute. Add the tins of chopped tomatoes and stir. Season with a pinch of salt and pepper. Reduce the heat and cook for a further 15–20 minutes.

4. Meanwhile, fill a large deep saucepan three-quarters full with water and add 1 tsp salt and 1 tsp olive oil and bring to the boil.

5. Very carefully place the spaghetti into the pan. The spaghetti will begin to bend with the heat of the water so it will all be covered by the water. Cook for about 10–12 minutes (check the instructions on the packet). The spaghetti should be soft but still have some 'bite'. When the spaghetti is cooked, drain using a colander.

6. Serve the spaghetti topped with some of the bolognaise sauce. Sprinkle on some grated cheese, if using.

Mango and lamb brochettes

500g/1lb lean boneless lamb

1 clove garlic, crushed

1cm/½in piece fresh ginger, peeled and grated

1 green chilli, deseeded and finely chopped

2 tsp mild curry powder

1 Tbsp tomato purée

3 Tbsp freshly squeezed lemon juice

6 Tbsp whole-milk plain yogurt

Salt and freshly ground black pepper

1 large ripe mango

For the salsa:

1 large ripe mango

1 small red onion, peeled and finely chopped

¼ cucumber, finely chopped

3 Tbsp mint, chopped

Serves 4

1. Wash and pat dry the lamb. Trim away any excess fat and then cut into 2.5cm/1in thick pieces and place in a bowl.

2. Mix together the garlic, ginger, chilli, curry powder, tomato purée, 1 Tbsp lemon juice and the yogurt. Season well. Mix into the lamb and coat well. Cover and chill for at least 2 hours.

3. Meanwhile, peel the skin from the mangoes. Slice down either side of the smooth flat central stone and cut the flesh from the mango into 2.5cm/1in pieces. Cover and chill until required.

4. To make the salsa, finely chop the flesh from the second mango and mix together the onion, cucumber and mint. Cover and chill until required.

5. Thread the lamb with pieces of mango alternately on to eight skewers and arrange on a grill rack. Brush with any yogurt mixture that remains in the bowl.

6. Preheat the grill to moderate, and cook the skewers for about 15 minutes, turning occasionally, until tender and slightly pink, or cook longer until cooked to your liking. Serve the skewers with the prepared salsa.

Creamy pork with mushrooms and peppers

2 Tbsp sunflower oil

500g/1lb pork steaks, cut into thin strips

1 large onion, peeled and thinly sliced

1 garlic clove, peeled and crushed

175g/6oz mushrooms, sliced or quartered

1 red pepper, deseeded and sliced

1 orange or yellow pepper, deseeded and sliced

1 Tbsp tomato purée

2 Tbsp peanut butter (smooth or crunchy)

150ml/¼ pt chicken stock

200ml/7fl oz crème fraîche or double cream

Salt and freshly ground black pepper

2 Tbsp snipped fresh chives

Serves 4

1. Heat 1 tablespoon of the oil in a wok and stir-fry the pork in two batches over a brisk heat for 5 minutes each batch or until the strips are lightly browned. Drain from the wok and set aside.

2. Add the rest of the oil to the wok, lower the heat and add the onion. Cover and fry for 5 minutes until starting to soften, then remove the lid and add the garlic, mushrooms and peppers. Increase the heat to medium and fry the vegetables for 5 minutes, stirring frequently.

3. Add the tomato purée and peanut butter, return the pork and any juices from it to the wok and stir in the stock. Bring to the boil, then lower the heat and simmer for 5 minutes.

4. Stir in the crème fraîche or double cream and season to taste. Simmer for a further 2 minutes, sprinkle with the chives and serve immediately.

Warm pasta salad

300g/10oz pasta

2 Tbsp olive oil

Pinch of salt

150g/5oz of any of the following: pancetta, salami, cooked bacon bits, cooked chicken, pepperoni (any cooked meat can be used)

½ onion, peeled and chopped

1 garlic clove, peeled and chopped or crushed

50g/2oz peppers, chopped (any colours are fine)

2 Tbsp sweetcorn

50g/2oz baby tomatoes, quartered

2 Tbsp peas

2 spring onions (scallions), chopped

3 Tbsp chopped fresh herbs (e.g. parsley, basil or chives)

200ml/7fl oz cream

50g/2oz grated cheese (Cheddar or Parmesan)

Serves 4

1. Put the pasta into a large saucepan with 1 tbsp olive oil and a pinch of salt. Add enough boiling water to the pan to cover the pasta. Set over a medium heat and cook according to the packet instructions. When the pasta is cooked, drain using the colander.

2. Heat 1 tbsp oil in a large pan and add the cooked meat. Cook gently for 1–2 minutes. Add the onion, garlic and peppers and cook for a further minute.

3. Reduce the heat to low. Add the sweetcorn, tomatoes, peas, spring onions (scallions), herbs and the cream. Cook for 1–2 minutes or until the cream has thickened.

4. Add the cooked pasta and then increase the heat. Cook, stirring, for about one minute. Remove from the heat, sprinkle the cheese over the top and serve immediately.

Cajun hash browns with chorizo and cherry tomatoes

700g/1lb waxy potatoes
(e.g. Desirée)

2 Tbsp sunflower oil

2 chorizo sausages, cut into
bite-sized pieces

1 red pepper, deseeded and
chopped

1 orange pepper, deseeded
and chopped

6 spring onions, trimmed and
chopped

75g/3oz butter

1 tsp Cajun seasoning, or
to taste

12 cherry tomatoes, halved

2 Tbsp chopped fresh parsley

Serves 4

1. Peel the potatoes and cut into even-sized chunks.
Boil in a pan of water (you can use a wok for this as
long as it is flat-bottomed or you have a wok burner)
until just tender. Drain and coarsely crush or chop them
into small pieces. (Carefully dry the wok if you have
used it to boil the potatoes.)

2. Heat the oil in the wok, add the chorizo pieces and fry
for 5 minutes over a medium heat. Add the peppers and
spring onions and fry for a further 5 minutes. Remove from
the wok and set aside.

3. Add the butter to the wok and, when melted, tip in the
potatoes and sprinkle over the Cajun seasoning. Fry for
10 minutes until golden brown, stirring and turning the
pieces over occasionally. Stir in the chorizo, peppers, spring
onions and cherry tomato halves. Fry for a further
5 minutes until the potatoes are crisp and the chorizo
and vegetables are piping hot. Sprinkle with the parsley
and serve.

Pasta carbonara

300g/10½oz dried white
   or wholemeal pasta shapes,
   e.g. wheels or bows

3 eggs

3 Tbsp crème fraîche or
   single (light) cream

50g/2oz Parmesan cheese or
   Cheddar cheese, finely
   grated

1 Tbsp chopped fresh parsley

Salt and freshly ground black
   pepper

50g/2oz cooked sliced
   ham, cut into thin strips

Serves 4

1. Cook the pasta in a large pan of lightly salted boiling water for 10 minutes, or according to packet instructions, until 'al dente'.

2. Meanwhile, lightly whisk the eggs together with a fork. Add the crème fraîche or single cream, half the cheese, parsley and a little pepper, if liked. Whisk again.

3. As soon as the pasta is cooked, turn off the heat, drain the pasta thoroughly and return to the hot pan. Immediately add the egg mixture with the strips of ham. Toss the mixture together well; the eggs will cook in the residual heat to make a sauce. Serve straight away, sprinkled with the remaining cheese.

Plum duck with stir-fried vegetables

4 duck breasts, skinned if preferred

Freshly ground black pepper

4 Tbsp groundnut oil

2 carrots, peeled and sliced

8 spring onions, trimmed and sliced

200g/8oz baby corn, chopped

200g/8oz mushrooms, sliced

8 cherry tomatoes, halved

2 Tbsp light soy sauce

6 Tbsp stir-fry plum sauce

2 Tbsp rice vinegar

2 tsp sesame seeds

Serves 4

1. Season the duck with freshly ground black pepper. Heat a wok over a medium heat, add the duck and cook for 7–8 minutes or until the breasts are done to your liking, turning them over once or twice.

2. Drain the duck from the wok and set aside for 5 minutes before slicing as thinly as possible. Pour off the fat and carefully wipe out the wok with absorbent kitchen paper.

3. Heat the oil in the wok, add the carrot and stir-fry over a medium-high heat for 3 minutes. Add the spring onions, corn and mushrooms and stir-fry for 3 minutes. Add the cherry tomato halves and stir-fry for a further 2 minutes.

4. Combine the soy sauce, plum sauce and rice vinegar and pour over the vegetables. Add the duck and toss everything over the heat for 1–2 minutes until coated in the sauce. Serve at once with the sesame seeds scattered over.

Asparagus, bacon and cherry tomato pizza

1 x 30-cm/12in Crispy pizza base (see page 13)

5 slices bacon, chopped into 2cm/¾in pieces or 50g/2oz pancetta, cubed

200g/7oz mozzarella, sliced

150g/5oz fresh asparagus, woody stems removed, chopped

200g/7oz cherry tomatoes, halved

50g/2oz goat's cheese, crumbled

Freshly ground black pepper

Chilli oil

Makes 1 pizza

1. Prepare the pizza base so it is ready to be topped. Preheat the oven to 220°C/425°F/Gas mark 7.

2. Put the cubes of bacon in a large frying pan and set over medium-high heat. Cook until the fat is released and the bacon is just browned. Remove the bacon with a slotted spoon and drain on absorbent kitchen paper.

3. Place mozzarella slices over the base leaving a 1–2cm/½–¾in border uncovered around the edge. Top with bacon slices, chopped asparagus and cherry tomatoes. Finish with crumbled goat's cheese and pepper to taste. Bake for 12–14 minutes, until the crust is golden and the base is cooked through in the centre. Remove from the oven, drizzle with chilli oil and serve immediately.

Capricciosa

1 x 30-cm/12-in Crispy pizza
base (see page 13)

350g/12oz mixed ripe
tomatoes

⅛ tsp salt

1 clove garlic, crushed

1 small white onion, thinly
sliced

100g/3½oz chestnut
mushrooms, thinly sliced

50g/2oz pepperoni slices

50g/2oz salami slices

50g/2oz prosciutto slices

50g/2oz black olives

150g/5oz mozzarella, sliced

Sea salt and freshly ground
black pepper

Makes 1 pizza

1. Prepare the pizza base so it is ready to be topped.
Preheat the oven to 220°C/425°F/Gas mark 7.

2. Roughly chop the tomatoes and place in a sieve over
a bowl. Press the tomatoes firmly with the back of a spoon
to release as much liquid as possible. Sprinkle with salt
(and a pinch of sugar if the tomatoes aren't very sweet)
and leave to drain for a further 10 minutes.

3. Spoon the tomatoes over the base, leaving about
1–2cm/½–¾in uncovered around the edge, and sprinkle
with crushed garlic. Top with the remaining ingredients
and season with sea salt and pepper to taste. Bake for
10–12 minutes, or until the cheese has melted and the
crust is golden. Serve immediately.

Make your own pizza party

1 quantity Quick scone base dough or Gluten-free quick pizza base dough (see pages 14)

Quick classic tomato sauce (see page 24)

Shop-bought barbecue sauce

All, or a selection, of the following toppings

Frankfurters, chopped into bite-sized pieces

Salami, thinly sliced

Cooked chicken breasts or ham, chopped

1 green pepper, cored and sliced into rings

1 red pepper, cored and sliced into rings

1 small pineapple, chopped into bite-sized pieces

Gouda, harvarti or Cheddar cheese, grated

Sweetcorn

Cherry tomatoes, sliced or halved

Makes 4 x 15cm/6in pizzas

1. Preheat the oven to 220°C/425°F/Gas mark 7. Divide the pizza dough into four balls. Roll the balls, one at a time on a floured surface, into 15cm/6in rounds. Place the sauces and the topping ingredients in individual bowls.

2. Allow children to top their own pizzas with their chosen ingredients. Transfer the pizzas to baking sheets lined with baking parchment and bake for 6–8 minutes, until the crust is golden and the cheese is bubbling. Allow to cool slightly, slice and serve.

Fish

Mustard-spiced prawns and monkfish

2 Tbsp sunflower or soya oil

2 or 3 cloves garlic, finely chopped or puréed

250g/9oz white onion paste (see page 23)

about 200ml/7fl oz water

350g/12oz monkfish flesh, cut into bite-sized pieces

350g/12oz raw king prawns, weighed after peeling and removing the heads, tails and veins

1 or 2 tsp chopped dried red chillies

1 or 2 green chillies, finely chopped

sugar, to taste (optional)

salt, to taste

Masala 1:

2 tablespoons mustard powder

½ teaspoon chilli powder

½ teaspoon turmeric

¼ fenugreek seeds, ground

Masala 2:

1 teaspoon nigella (wild onion) seeds

1 teaspoon turmeric

1 teaspoon black mustard seeds

Garnish:

2 or 3 dried red chillies, whole

white poppy seeds, to sprinkle

Serves 4

1. Mix enough water with Masala 1 to make a smooth paste.

2. Heat the oil in a karahi or wok. Add Masala 2 and stir-fry for 15 seconds. Add the garlic and stir-fry for about 30 seconds, then add the onion paste and stir-fry for 1 minute.

3. Stir in the water and, when simmering, add the monkfish, prawns, dried and fresh chillies.

4. Simmer for about 10 minutes or until cooked. Season with salt and a little sugar, if using, then garnish with the whole dried red chillies and some poppy seeds before serving.

Salmon with sun-blush tomatoes

3 Tbsp olive oil

2 spring onions, finely sliced

2 garlic cloves, finely chopped

450g/1lb salmon, skinned and cut into chunks

400g/14oz tinned cannellini beans

Grated rind of 1 lemon

1 tsp paprika

55g/2oz sun-blush tomatoes, roughly chopped

125g/5oz wild rocket

Salt and freshly ground black pepper, to season

Extra virgin olive oil, for drizzling

Serves 3–4

1. Heat a large frying pan or wok and when hot add the oil. Add the spring onions and garlic and stir-fry for 2 minutes, making sure you don't burn the garlic. Add the salmon and gently stir-fry the fish for 5 minutes. Remove, set aside and keep warm. Re-heat the pan and add the beans, lemon rind, paprika and sun-blush tomatoes. Stir-fry for 2 minutes until heated through.

2. Gently stir in the rocket and season with salt and freshly ground black pepper. Serve with the fish. Drizzle with a little extra virgin olive oil.

Cod and haddock fishcakes

250g/9oz cod, cooked
and flaked

200g/7oz haddock, cooked
and flaked

350g/12oz mashed
potatoes

Salt and freshly ground
black pepper

25g/1oz butter, melted

1 Tbsp freshly chopped
chives

2 eggs, beaten

3 Tbsp white breadcrumbs

4 Tbsp sunflower oil for frying

Serves 4

1. Mix together the fish, potatoes and seasoning. Add the melted butter, chopped chives and enough egg to bind together – not too wet. Leave to cool in the fridge for 30 minutes.

2. Using wet hands, shape the mixture into 8 flat cakes. Dip the cakes in the remaining beaten egg and then into the breadcrumbs to coat.

3. Heat half the oil in a frying pan and cook 4 fishcakes for about 4–5 minutes on either side, until golden. Repeat with the remaining oil and fishcakes and serve immediately with lemon wedges and a crisp green salad.

Grilled garlic red mullet

4 whole red mullet, about 30 cm/12 inches long, gutted, cleaned and dried

juice of 2 limes

1 tsp salt

2 tsp finely chopped fresh red chillies

8 cloves garlic

175g/6oz raw cashew nuts, chopped

1 Tbsp coarsely chopped fresh coriander

2 or 3 green chillies, chopped

1 Tbsp sesame oil

Garnish:

lime wedges

dark salad leaves

Serves 4

1. Using a small, sharp knife, make several slashes on the sides of the fish. Mix the lime juice, salt and red chillies together. Coat the fish, inside and out with this mixture, cover and refrigerate for 1 hour or so.

2. Put the garlic, cashews, coriander, green chillies and oil in a blender or food processor and 'pulse', using water as needed, to a smooth and pourable paste. Rub the paste into both sides of the fish, retaining any spare paste.

3. To cook, place the fish on a rack in a grill pan lined with foil to catch drips. Cook under a preheated medium grill for 8–10 minutes. Turn the fish, baste with any remaining marinade and grill for a further 5–8 minutes. Serve garnished with lime wedges and salad leaves.

Tuna and bean salad

450g/1lb fresh tuna, cut into chunks

250g/9oz tinned butter beans

250g/9oz tinned cannellini beans

grated rind and juice of 2 lemons

5 Tbsp olive oil

1 small bunch flat-leaf parsley, leaves only

1 bunch chives, chopped

1 baby red Cos lettuce

salt and pepper

Serves 6

1. Heat the griddle pan until smoking then add the tuna and cook until marked on both sides. Do not over-cook – you want to keep the tuna rare in the middle. Set aside.

2. Drain the beans and rinse under running cold water. Place the beans in a bowl, add the lemon juice, oil, herbs and lettuce then the tuna.

3. Gently toss with your hands and put on a plate. Season and serve.

Prawns with minted chilli and orange sauce

2 bunch of fresh coriander

4 garlic cloves, peeled and roughly chopped

2 tsp grated fresh ginger or ginger purée

6 Tbsp vegetable oil

700g/24oz large, raw prawns, peeled, with tails left on

300ml/½pt fresh orange juice

4 Tbsp light soy sauce

2 tsp cornflour

2 red chillies, deseeded and finely sliced

2 Tbsp chopped fresh mint

150g/6oz green beans, halved lengthways

200g/8oz small Asian mushrooms (e.g. shimeji or enoki) or baby button mushrooms

3 cherry tomatoes, halved

Serves 4

1. Remove any tough stalks from the coriander and put the rest of the bunch in a food processor with the garlic, ginger and 1 tablespoon of the oil and blend to a smooth purée. Spread the coriander mixture over the prawns and leave to marinate in the fridge for 1 hour.

2. In a small bowl, mix together the orange juice, soy sauce and cornflour until smooth. Stir in the chilli and chopped mint. Set aside.

3. Heat the remaining oil in a wok, add the green beans and mushrooms stir-fry over a high heat for 3 minutes. Add the prawns and any marinade left in the dish and stir-fry for 2 minutes. Add the cherry tomatoes and stir-fry for a further 1 minute or until the prawns turn pink.

4. Pour in the orange sauce mixture and stir until thickened. Simmer for 30 seconds and serve immediately with rice.

Mediterranean fish stew

2 Tbsp olive oil

1 red onion, peeled and
chopped

2 garlic cloves, peeled and
chopped

½ green pepper, deseeded
and chopped

1 courgette, chopped

350g/12oz potatoes, peeled
and cut into chunks

Few strands of saffron

1 tsp smoked paprika

150ml/¼pt dry white wine

400g/14oz tin chopped
tomatoes

1 Tbsp shredded fresh basil

500g/1lb 2oz white fish fillets,
skinned and cut into
2.5cm/1in pieces

225g/8oz raw prawns,
peeled

Salt and freshly ground black
pepper

Serves 4

1. Heat the oil in a wok, add the onion and fry gently
for 5 minutes. Add the garlic, green pepper, courgette
and potatoes and fry for a further 5 minutes, stirring
occasionally.

2. Crumble the saffron over the vegetables and add the
smoked paprika. Fry for 2 minutes, then add the wine,
tomatoes and basil. Simmer for 15 minutes or until the
potatoes are almost tender, the tomatoes have reduced
and the sauce thickened.

3. Add the fish and prawns and season to taste. Simmer
for a further 5 minutes until all the fish is cooked.
Serve immediately.

Salmon steamed with lemongrass, lime and basil

4 x 150g/5oz salmon fillets

1 small knob of fresh ginger, peeled and cut into fine shreds

1 stalk of lemongrass, quartered lengthways

2 Tbsp chopped fresh basil

Finely grated zest of 1 lime

About 450ml/¾pt fish stock or water

4 spring onions, trimmed

200g/7oz tenderstem broccoli

1 carrot, peeled and cut into julienne

For the sauce:

2 Tbsp Thai fish sauce

1 tsp light brown sugar

2 Tbsp light soy sauce

Juice of 1 lime

½ stalk of lemongrass, finely sliced

Serves 4

1. Place the salmon fillets on to a steaming rack and sprinkle over the ginger, lemongrass, half the basil and lime zest.

2. Pour the stock into the wok so it is one-third full. Tuck the spring onions, broccoli and carrot around the salmon on the rack. Bring the stock to a simmer, cover the wok with a lid and steam for 10 minutes or until the salmon flesh flakes easily and the vegetables are cooked.

3. For the sauce, mix all the ingredients together, stirring until the sugar dissolves. Place the salmon and vegetables on serving plates and drizzle over the sauce. Garnish with the rest of the chopped basil.

Minted monkfish spiedini

450g/1lb monkfish tail,
  boned and cleaned

1 red and 1 yellow ramiro
  pepper

olive oil

juice of 2 lemons

1 clove garlic, crushed

1 bunch mint, leaves only

salt and pepper

1 lemon, cut into wedges

serves 6

1. Heat the griddle pan on the hob until smoking.

2. Cut the monkfish and the peppers into bite-sized chunks. Mix the olive oil, lemon juice and garlic together. Brush the monkfish and pepper chunks with the mixture.

3. Lay the monkfish and peppers on the griddle in batches and cook on each side until scored. Repeat until all the chunks are cooked.

4. Skewer the chunks alternately with a mint leaf, monkfish, yellow pepper, mint leaf, monkfish, red pepper and so on. Season and serve with a wedge of lemon.

Fish with tahini sauce and walnuts

For the fish:

1kg/2lb 3oz white fish fillet, such as snapper, grouper, cod or hake

4 Tbsp olive oil

4 medium onions, peeled and chopped

5 garlic cloves, peeled and crushed

90g/3oz fresh coriander, chopped

2 medium tomatoes, chopped

1 hot chilli, chopped

1 Tbsp tomato purée

125g/4oz walnuts, chopped

2 Tbsp pine nuts

For the sauce:

60ml/2fl oz tahini

60ml/2fl oz lemon juice

60ml/2fl oz water

Salt and black pepper, to taste

Bread, to serve

Serves 4–5

1. Preheat the oven to 200°C/400°F/Gas Mark 6. Start by preparing the fish. Rinse the fillets and pat dry with absorbent kitchen paper. Place them in a greased oven-proof dish and cook in the oven for about 25 minutes, until tender.

2. Heat 2 tablespoons olive oil in a frying pan and fry the onions until golden brown. Add the garlic, coriander, tomatoes, chilli and tomato paste. Bring to the boil for 2 minutes, then remove from heat.

3. To make the tahini sauce, combine all the sauce ingredients together. Add the sauce to the pan with the onion mixture and return to the heat, stirring continuously until it starts to boil. Remove from heat.

4. In a separate frying pan, brown the walnuts in 2 tablespoons olive oil, then remove from the heat. Add the pine nuts to the oil and brown.

5. To serve, place the fish fillet on a platter, top with the tahini sauce and garnish with the walnuts and pine nuts. Serve with bread.

Spinach pancakes with haddock

250g/8oz spinach, trimmed

1 quantity Basic pancake batter (see page 26), unsweetened

350g/12oz smoked haddock fillet

600ml/20fl oz milk

1 bay leaf

1 quantity Basic savoury white sauce (see page 24)

125g/4oz Gruyère cheese, grated

2 Tbsp finely chopped fresh chives

Salt and ground black pepper

2 large eggs, hard-boiled and chopped

Tomato, black olive, garlic and basil salsa (See page 22), to serve

Serves 4

1. Wash the spinach leaves and pack into a saucepan while still wet. Cover the pan with a lid and cook the spinach over gentle heat for about 5 minutes, until wilted. Drain well, pressing against the sides of a colander to extract as much water as possible. Allow the spinach to cool and then chop finely.

2. Prepare the batter and stir in the spinach. Make the pancakes and keep warm. Wash and pat dry the haddock and place in a shallow pan with a lid. Pour over the milk and add the bay leaf. Bring to the boil, cover and simmer gently for about 5 minutes until cooked through. Drain, reserving the milk to make the white sauce. Discard the bay leaf.

3. Remove the skin from the haddock and flake the flesh. Cover and keep warm. Make the white sauce and stir in the cheese and chives. Season and stir in the haddock and egg. Heat through gently for about 3 minutes until piping hot then fill the pancakes with the mixture. Serve with the salsa.

Mackerel with sweet and sour plum relish

4 tsp wholegrain mustard

2 Tbsp runny honey

8 x 100g/3½oz mackerel fillets

2 Tbsp balsamic vinegar

2 tsp sesame oil

Salt and freshly ground black pepper

250g/8oz ripe plums, halved, stoned and finely chopped

1 medium red or yellow pepper, deseeded and finely chopped

4 spring onions, trimmed and finely chopped

1 medium carrot, peeled and grated

60g/2oz beansprouts, roughly chopped

To serve:
Crusty bread

Serves 4

1. Mix together the mustard and 1 tablespoon of honey. Wash and pat dry the mackerel fillets and season on both sides.

2. Preheat the grill to medium. Arrange the mackerel fillets on the grill rack, flesh-side up, and brush with the mustard and honey. Cook for 5 to 6 minutes, without turning, until tender and cooked through. Drain and set aside while you prepare the relish.

3. Mix the remaining honey with the vinegar and sesame oil and season well. Place the remaining ingredients in a bowl and mix in the vinegar and oil dressing.

4. While the mackerel is still warm, flake it from the skin. Arrange the relish on serving plates and top with the mackerel. Serve with crusty bread.

Salmon and herb waffles

500g/1lb salmon fillets

2 bay leaves

210ml/7fl oz dry white wine

1 quantity Basic waffle batter (see page 27), unsweetened

3 Tbsp chopped dill

3 Tbsp chopped tarragon

2½ Tbsp+1 tsp cornflour

Salt and freshly ground black pepper

180g/6oz smoked salmon pieces

6 Tbsp single cream

3 Tbsp finely chopped chives

Fresh dill, to garnish

Serves 6

1. Wash and pat dry the salmon fillets and place in a large shallow pan with a lid. Add the bay leaves and wine, and about 450ml/15fl oz water to just cover the fish. Bring to the boil, cover and simmer gently for about 8 minutes, until just cooked through. Set aside to cool. Prepare the waffle batter (see page 27), adding the dill and tarragon. Cook and keep warm.

2. Drain the salmon, reserving the stock, and discard the skin and bay leaves. Flake the salmon and set aside. Strain the stock through a sieve into a jug, and reserve 600ml/20fl oz.

3. Place the cornflour in a saucepan and add a little of the reserved stock. Mix to form a paste and then pour in the remaining stock. Bring to the boil, stirring, and cook for 1 minute, Remove from the heat and stir in the seasoning, smoked salmon, cream and chives, then carefully mix in the cooked, flaked salmon. Return to the heat and heat through gently for about 5 minutes until piping hot, taking care not to boil. Pile the salmon mixture on top of the waffles and serve garnished with dill.

Cod Provençal

4 x 150g/5oz cod fillets, skinned

1 tsp paprika

1 tsp herbes de Provence

4 Tbsp extra-virgin olive oil

1 red pepper, deseeded and cut into wedges

1 yellow pepper, deseeded and cut into wedges

1 courgette, sliced

2 garlic cloves, peeled and thinly sliced

4 small tomatoes or 8 cherry tomatoes, halved

4 anchovy fillets, snipped into small pieces

75g/3oz black olives

Juice of 1 lemon

Few fresh basil leaves, shredded

Freshly ground black pepper

Serves 4

1. Dust the cod fillets with the paprika and dried herbs and set aside.

2. Heat half the oil in a wok and fry the red and yellow pepper wedges, the courgette slices and garlic over a medium-high heat for 6–8 minutes or until lightly browned. Add the tomatoes and stir-fry for a further 2 minutes. Remove from the wok and keep warm in a low oven.

3. Heat the rest of the oil in the wok, add the cod and scatter over the chopped anchovies and black olives. Fry over a medium heat for 5 minutes, then carefully turn the fish over and fry for a further 3–4 minutes or until cooked.

4. Divide the vegetables between serving plates and top with the cod, anchovies and olives. Stir the lemon juice into the wok and as soon as it bubbles, spoon the cooking juices over the fish.

5. Garnish with the shredded basil, season with black pepper; serve with new or sauté potatoes.

Prawns
with mango

675g/1lb 6oz raw king
  prawns, weighed after
  peeling and removing the
  heads but leaving the tails on

4 Tbsp sunflower oil

4–6 cloves garlic, finely
  chopped

150g/5oz onion, thinly
  sliced

4 or more green chillies,
  shredded

200ml/7fl oz tinned
  coconut milk

1–2 firm fresh mangoes,
  peeled and the flesh cut
  into thin strips

10–12 fresh or dried curry
  leaves (optional)

2 Tbsp fresh lime juice

salt, to taste

fresh coriander, to garnish

Serves 4

1. Inspect the prawns, remove the veins from their backs using a sharp knife and rinse them clean.

2. Heat the oil in a large frying pan. Add the garlic, onion and chillies and stir-fry for about 5 minutes.

3. Add the coconut milk, mango strips and curry leaves, if using, and, when simmering over a low heat, add the prawns. Cook for 8–12 minutes, depending on prawn size, turning once or twice. During this time, the coconut milk will reduce in volume, so compensate for this by adding water, little by little, to keep the mixture loose.

4. Sprinkle the lime juice over the top and season with salt. Garnish with the coriander and serve with rice.

Red-braised fillets of Sea Bass

1 tsp ginger purée

1 garlic clove, peeled and
  crushed

1 Tbsp light soy sauce

1 Tbsp rice wine or dry sherry

1 tsp sweet chilli sauce

3 Tbsp yellow bean sauce

100ml/3½fl oz fish stock

1 tsp brown sugar

4 x 175g/6oz sea bass fillets

2 Tbsp groundnut or
  sunflower oil

2 tsp sesame oil

To garnish:

1 large carrot, peeled and
  cut into julienne

2 spring onions, shredded

1 Tbsp tinned bamboo
  shoots, shredded

2 Tbsp chopped fresh chives

Serves 4

1. In a small bowl, mix together the ginger, garlic, soy
sauce, rice wine or sherry, chilli sauce, yellow bean
sauce, fish stock and sugar, stirring until the sugar
dissolves and the ingredients are evenly mixed.

2. Rinse the fish fillets and pat dry with absorbent kitchen
paper. With a knife, cut several slashes through the skin of
each fillet.

3. Heat the oil in a wok, add two fillets skin-side down and
cook over a medium heat for 3 minutes. Turn them over
and cook for a further 1 minute, then drain and set aside.
Cook the other two fillets in the same way and set aside.

4. Sprinkle the fish with the sesame oil. Pour the sauce
mix into the wok and bring to a simmer. Return the fish to
the wok, basting the fillets with the sauce. Cook gently for
5 minutes, turning the fish over halfway or spooning the
sauce over the fillets regularly.

5. Serve garnished with the shredded vegetables and
chives and accompany with egg noodles or rice.

Walnut pesto and hot-smoked salmon pizza

1 x 30cm/12in Crispy pizza base (see page 13)

2 Tbsp Walnut pesto (see page 20)

2 Tbsp crème fraîche

150g/5oz hot-smoked salmon

1 small chicory, finely shredded (optional)

100g/3½oz mozzarella, sliced

Salt and freshly ground black pepper

50g/2oz watercress

Extra virgin olive oil

Makes 1 pizza

1. Prepare the pizza base so it ready to be topped. Preheat the oven to 220°C/425°F/Gas mark 7.

2. Combine the Walnut pesto and crème fraîche and spread evenly over the base, leaving about a 2-cm/3⁄4-in border uncovered around the edge. Scatter over the hot smoked salmon, chicory, if using, and mozzarella. Season generously with salt and freshly ground black pepper.

3. Cook in the middle of the preheated oven for 10–12 minutes or until golden and crispy. Remove from the oven, sprinkle over the watercress, drizzle with extra virgin olive oil and serve immediately.

Jambalaya pancakes

1 quantity Basic pancake batter (see page 26), unsweetened, made with 300ml/10fl oz buttermilk

2 Tbsp sun-dried tomato purée

¼ tsp garlic powder

1 Tbsp vegetable oil

1 medium onion, chopped

2 stalks celery, trimmed and chopped, and leaves, reserved for garnish

1 small red pepper, deseeded and chopped

1 small green pepper, deseeded and chopped

1 tsp Cajun spice seasoning

400g/14oz tin chopped tomatoes

250g/8oz cooked, lean chicken, chopped

125g/4oz large, peeled prawns, defrosted if frozen

Salt and freshly ground black pepper

Serves 4

1. Prepare the pancake batter (See page 26), replacing the milk with buttermilk. Stir the tomato paste and garlic powder into the batter, and cook as directed. Keep warm.

2. Heat the oil in a large frying pan and gently fry the onion, celery and peppers for about 5 minutes until softened but not browned. Add the Cajun seasoning and tomatoes, bring to the boil and simmer for 20 minutes, until tender.

3. Stir the cooked chicken and prawns into the mixture and heat through for about 5 minutes until piping hot. Season to taste. Pile the jambalaya filling onto each pancake and fold over. Serve two per person, sprinkled with reserved celery leaves.

Cod with chilli soy vegetables

For the marinade:

1 red chilli, deseeded and finely chopped

2 tsp sesame oil

Juice of 1 lemon

1 Tbsp soy sauce

450g/1lb firm white fish, e.g. cod or haddock, skinned and cut into bite-sized pieces

For the stir fry:

2 Tbsp vegetable oil

1 red chilli, deseeded and finely chopped

2cm/1in fresh ginger, peeled and grated

2 garlic cloves, finely sliced

120g/4oz baby corn

110g/3½oz fresh or frozen peas

110g/3½oz beansprouts

2 spring onions, finely sliced

To serve:
Toasted sesame noodles

Serves 4

1. In a medium-sized bowl mix the marinade ingredients together and add the fish. Cover and refrigerate for 5 minutes.

2. Heat a large frying pan or wok and add the oil. When it is hot, add the chilli, ginger and garlic, and stir-fry for 1 minute.

3. Add the baby corn, peas, beansprouts and spring onions and stir-fry for 2 minutes. Remove and keep warm. Bring the wok back up to the heat, remove the fish from the marinade and add to the pan. Stir-fry gently for a further 2 minutes until the fish is opaque and cooked through. Serve with the vegetables and toasted sesame noodles.

Crispy tuna with sweet chilli vegetables

450g/1lb tuna steak, skinned and cut into bite-sized chunks

2 tsp cornflour

2 Tbsp vegetable oil

2 red onions, sliced

2 red peppers, finely sliced

2 small heads pak choy

1 Tbsp soy sauce

1 Tbsp sweet chilli sauce

1 Tbsp sake (optional)

1 Tbsp lime juice

2 tsp runny honey

1 small bunch fresh mint, roughly chopped

Serves 4

1. Toss the tuna in the cornflour and shake off any excess. Heat a large frying pan or wok and add the oil. Stir-fry the tuna in batches, for 5 minutes per batch. When each batch is cooked, remove and drain on absorbent kitchen paper. Set aside.

2. Wipe the pan and re-heat. When hot and slightly smoking, stir-fry the onion and peppers for 5 minutes until soft. Add the soy sauce, chilli sauce, sake (if using), lime juice, honey and pak choy, and stir-fry for 1 minute until hot and the pak choi has wilted. Tip into a serving dish, top with the crispy tuna and scatter over the mint.

Salmon, dill and fresh pea pasta

340g/12oz dried spaghetti

Olive oil, for sprinkling

2 Tbsp vegetable oil

2 garlic cloves, finely chopped

450g/1lb salmon fillet, skinned and cut into chunks

225g/8oz fresh or frozen peas

1 small bunch dill

1 small bunch mint

4 spring onions, finely sliced

Grated rind and juice of 1 lemon

2 Tbsp extra virgin oil, for drizzling

4 Tbsp Parmesan cheese, to serve

Serves 3-4

1. Heat a large pan of lightly salted water. When boiling, add the pasta and cook for 8–10 minutes. Drain and run under cold water. Sprinkle with olive oil and set aside.

2. Heat the oil in a large frying pan or wok and add the garlic. Stir-fry for 30 seconds making sure the garlic does not burn. Add the salmon and cook, without moving it around the pan, for 2 minutes. Turn the salmon over and cook for a further 2 minutes. Remove and keep warm.

3. Meanwhile, add the peas, pasta, dill, mint, spring onions and lemon rind and mix well. Stir-fry for 2 minutes until heated through. Return the salmon to the pan. Sprinkle over the lemon juice and drizzle with olive oil. Grate over a little Parmesan cheese.

Quick kedgeree

150ml/5fl oz milk

2 bay leaves

450g/1lb smoked haddock

2 Tbsp groundnut oil

4 cardamom seeds, crushed

1 Tbsp garam masala

2 tsp turmeric

1 tsp ground coriander

2 cloves

1 onion, finely chopped

1 x 1cm/½in fresh ginger, peeled and grated

1 green chilli, deseeded and finely chopped

285g/10oz cooked basmati rice

2 Tbsp fresh parsley, chopped

Salt and freshly ground black pepper, to season

To serve:

2 hard-boiled eggs, shelled and cut into quarters

Lemon wedges

Serves 3–4

1. Put the milk in a pan large enough to hold the fish, then add the bay leaves and smoked haddock, bring to a simmer and poach for 5 minutes. Strain, cool and flake the fish into bite-sized pieces.

2. Heat a large frying pan or wok, add the oil, cardamom seeds, garam masala, turmeric, coriander and cloves. Stir-fry for 1 minute and then add the onion, ginger and chilli. Cook for a further 5 minutes. Add the cooked rice and stir well to combine all the ingredients.

3. Add the flaked fish, stir into the rice and cook for another 2 minutes until the fish is heated through. Scatter over the parsley and season with salt and freshly ground black pepper. Serve with the quartered hard-boiled eggs and lemon wedges.

Mackerel salad

For the salad:

1 crisphead lettuce

2 handfuls of fresh rocket leaves

12 sprigs of dill, chopped

4 mackerel

700ml/24fl oz sunflower oil

2 Tbsp olive oil for frying

2 tsp pine nuts

2 large tomato, peeled, deseeded and sliced

2 Tbsp currants, soaked

For the dressing:

125ml/4fl oz olive oil

Juice of 1 lemon

1 tsp mustard

2 tsp white wine vinegar

2 Tbsp chicken stock

Pinch of salt and freshly ground black pepper

Serves 4

1. Start by preparing the salad. Rinse the lettuce and rocket and shred. Rinse the dill and remove the stalks.

2. Gut the mackerel, remove the gills and rinse thoroughly. Pat dry. Fry the mackerel in the sunflower oil and allow to cool before flaking.

3. Heat the olive oil in a pan and fry the pine nuts until golden brown.

4. Arrange the lettuce and rocket in a dome in the centre of a serving bowl. Place the slices of fish and tomato around the centre. Sprinkle the pine nuts, currants and chopped dill over the fish.

5. Prepare the dressing by mixing together the olive oil, lemon juice, mustard, vinegar, stock, salt and pepper, then drizzle over the salad.

Oven barbecued fish

1 whole perch, trout or carp weighing about 1.5kg/ 3lb 5 oz

4 Tbsp vegetable oil

3 large onions, peeled and thinly sliced

5 garlic cloves, peeled and crushed

1 tsp curry powder

1 tsp ground dried lime or grated rind of 1 lemon

2 tsp salt

2 Tbsp tamarind paste

250ml/9fl oz warm water

3 Tbsp parsley, chopped

3 Tbsp fresh coriander, chopped

Green salad, to serve

Serves 6

1. Clean and scale the fish. Cut it open lengthways from the head to the tail through the back. Rinse and pat dry with absorbent kitchen paper. Place the fish under the grill for 5 minutes on each side until partially cooked, then transfer to an oven-proof dish.

2. In the meantime, heat the vegetable oil in a frying pan. Fry the onions and garlic, stirring occasionally until tender. Stir in the curry powder, dried lime or lemon rind and salt.

3. Dissolve the tamarind paste in the warm water and add it to the onion mixture. Cook over a medium heat for 25 minutes, until it becomes a thick paste. Add the parsley and coriander.

4. Preheat the oven to 200°C/400°F/Gas Mark 6. Spread the onion mixture over the grilled fish. Cook in the oven for 15 to 20 minutes until the fish is cooked. Then place the fish under the grill for 1 minute until a thin crust has formed on the stuffing. Serve hot with a green salad.

Coriander pesto, prawn and feta pizza

1 x 30-cm/12-in Crispy pizza base (see page 13)

2 heaped Tbsp Coriander pesto (see page 21)

8–12 raw prawns, peeled

75g/2¾oz feta cheese, crumbled

Makes 1 pizza

1. Prepare the pizza base so it is ready to be topped. Preheat the oven to 220°C/425°F/Gas mark 7. Prepare the pesto and set aside.

2. Spoon the pesto over the pizza base leaving a 1–2cm/ ½–¾in border, uncovered around the edge. Top with prawns, turning to coat in pesto. Finish with crumbled feta. Bake for 10–12 minutes until the crust is golden. Serve immediately.

Salmon fish fingers with pea and potato mash

450g/1lb piece fresh salmon fillet, skinned

3 Tbsp plain flour

Salt and freshly ground black pepper, to taste

1 egg, lightly beaten

75g/2¾oz dry white breadcrumbs

2 tsp finely grated lemon zest (optional)

675g/24oz floury potatoes, peeled and cut into large chunks

200g/7oz frozen peas, defrosted

2 Tbsp semi-skimmed milk

25g/2 Tbsp sunflower margarine

1 Tbsp olive oil

Serves 4

1. Pat the fish fillet dry with absorbent kitchen paper, then place on a board and cut into eight fingers, each about 10 x 2.5cm/4 x 1in. Lightly season the flour with salt and pepper in a shallow bowl, lightly beat the egg in another bowl, and mix together the breadcrumbs and lemon zest in a third. Dip each piece of salmon first in the flour, shaking off the excess, then into the beaten egg and finally in the breadcrumbs. Place on a plate and chill until ready to cook.

2. Cook the potatoes in a large saucepan of lightly boiling water for 15 minutes, adding the peas for the last 2 minutes of cooking time. Drain thoroughly, then return to the pan with the milk and margarine and mash until smooth. Beat with a wooden spoon for a minute or two until fluffy.

3. While the potatoes and peas are cooking, heat the oil in a non-stick frying pan until hot. Add the salmon fingers, reduce the heat to medium and gently cook for 10 minutes, turning once until the outsides are golden brown and the salmon is just cooked. Serve straight away with the pea and potato mash. Adults may enjoy a wedge of lemon to squeeze over the salmon.

Veggie

Mixed vegetable curry

1 tsp turmeric

450g/1 lb peeled and trimmed vegetables of your choice, such as green beans, sweet potato, parsnips and carrots, cut into 1cm/ ½ inch cubes)

1 Tbsp mustard-blend oil

2 or 3 cloves garlic, finely sliced into rounds

150g/5oz finely chopped onion

10–12 fresh or dried curry leaves (optional)

2 green chillies, sliced lengthwise

water and flesh of 1 fresh coconut, the flesh shredded

salt, to taste

4 Tbsp caramelized onions, to garnish

Masala 1:

1 Tbsp split and polished black lentils (urid dhal)

1–2 tsp chopped dried red chillies

1 tsp black peppercorns

1 tsp cumin seeds

½ tsp black mustard seeds

½ tsp yellow mustard seeds

Masala 2:

1 tsp ground white pepper

1 tsp turmeric

½ tsp asafoetida

Serves 4

1. Dry-fry Masala 1 in a karahi or wok for about 30 seconds then set aside.

2. Bring plenty of water to the boil in a 2.25–2.75 litre/4–5 pint saucepan. Add the turmeric and the vegetables and simmer for about 5 minutes. Strain, retaining the cooking water.

3. Heat the oil in the karahi or wok. Add Masala 2 and stir-fry for 30 seconds, then add the garlic and stir-fry for another 30 seconds. Add the onion, curry leaves, if using, chillies and coconut flesh and water, and continue stir-frying for a further 1–2 minutes.

4. Add Masala 1 and the vegetables, together with enough of the retained cooking water to enable them to simmer without sticking.

5. When the vegetables are tender and heated through, season with salt. Heat the onion tarka then use it as a garnish. Serve at once with rice.

Aubergine and okra curry

2 large aubergines

1 Tbsp vegetable oil

1 quantity Thai chilli paste (see page 23)

100g/4oz okra, cut into thirds

4 large tomatoes, cut into large chunks or wedges

440ml/15fl oz tinned coconut milk

Juice of 1 lime

1 large handful fresh coriander leaves

Salt to taste

Freshly-cooked rice to serve

Extra chopped coriander, to garnish

Serves 4

1. Preheat the oven to 200°C/400°F/Gas mark 6. Lightly coat the aubergines in a little oil and place on a baking tray. Bake for 20–25 minutes or until soft but still holding their shape.

2. Heat the oil in a large frying pan. Add the Thai chilli paste and cook for 1–2 minutes until aromatic. Add the okra and cook for about 3 minutes. Then add the tomatoes and stir until they soften. Cut the aubergines into large chunks and add together with the coconut milk, reduce the heat and leave to simmer for 15–20 minutes or until the vegetables are tender. Remove from the heat and stir in the lime juice and coriander and season with salt to taste. Serve with freshly cooked rice and chopped coriander.

Thai green vegetable curry

2 tbsp vegetable oil

175g/6oz baby carrots, scrubbed

1 onion, peeled and chopped

175g/6oz (prepared weight) butternut squash, peeled, deseeded and cut into chunks

175g/6oz cauliflower florets

1 red pepper, deseeded and chopped

2 Tbsp Thai green curry paste

200ml/7fl oz vegetable stock

300ml/½ pt coconut milk

150g/5oz spinach leaves, shredded

Naan bread, to serve

Serves 4

1. Heat the oil in a wok, add the baby carrots and chopped onion and fry over a medium heat for 5 minutes. Add the chunks of squash, cauliflower florets and red pepper and fry for a further 5 minutes, stirring occasionally.

2. Stir in the curry paste and cook for 1 minute then pour in the stock. Lower the heat, cover the wok and simmer for 25 minutes or until the vegetables are tender.

3. Stir in the coconut milk and spinach and simmer for 2–3 minutes or until the spinach wilts. Serve with warm naan bread.

Pumpkin and sage pilaf

3 Tbsp groundnut oil

1kg/2lb pumpkin, peeled
  and cut into bite-size chunks

4 garlic cloves, thinly sliced

1 Tbsp chopped fresh sage

250g/9oz cooked basmati
  rice

75g/2½oz butter

1 tsp ground nutmeg

120g/4oz Parmesan cheese,
  grated

Freshly ground black pepper,
  to season

Deep fried sage leaves, to
  garnish

Serves 4

1. Heat a wok or a large frying pan. Add 2 Tbsp oil and stir-fry the pumpkin over a medium heat for 5 minutes. You may have to do this in batches depending on the size of your wok. Remove the pumpkin and keep warm.

2. Reheat the pan and add the remaining oil. Add the garlic and sage leaves and cook for a further 1 minute until golden and crisp.

3. Add the pumpkin, cooked rice, butter and nutmeg, and stir until all the ingredients are well combined and heated through. If the mixture is dry, add a little water. Sprinkle over the Parmesan cheese and freshly ground black pepper and serve with the deep fried sage leaves.

Moroccan vegetable tagine

150g/5oz dried apricots

150ml/2fl oz boiling water

2 Tbsp olive oil

1 onion, peeled and finely sliced

1½–2 Tbsp harissa paste (depending on taste)

½ tsp ground cinnamon

½ tsp ground cumin

2 parsnips (about 150g/5oz), peeled and cut into 2–3cm/ ¾–1¼in chunks

2 carrots (about 150g/5oz), peeled and cut into 2–3cm/ ¾–1¼in chunks

1 large sweet potato about 300–350g/10–12oz, peeled and cut into 2–3cm/¾–1¼in chunks

600g/1¼lb pumpkin or butternut squash, peeled and cut into 3cm/1¼in chunks

400g/14oz tin chickpeas, drained and rinsed

Salt to taste

50g/2oz flaked almonds, toasted

Small handful fresh coriander, roughly chopped

Serves 4–6

1. Put the apricots in a small bowl and pour over the water. Leave to soak while you prepare the rest of the tagine.

2. In a large, heavy-based saucepan heat the oil over medium heat. Add the onion and sauté for 2–3 minutes or until soft and translucent but not browned. Stir in the harissa, cinnamon and cumin. Then add the prepared vegetables and stir well until evenly coated. Cover and leave to cook over low-medium heat for 10 minutes, stirring occasionally.

3. Remove the lid and stir in the chickpeas, apricots and their soaking water and stir to combine. Cover again and continue to cook, stirring occasionally, for a further 20 minutes or until the vegetables are tender. Remove from the heat, season to taste and sprinkle over the almonds and coriander. Stir gently to combine then serve immediately.

Balti vegetables with mango

8 new potatoes, halved

2 carrots, peeled and sliced

175g/6oz small cauliflower florets

2 tbsp vegetable oil

1 onion, peeled and chopped

1 courgette, trimmed and chopped

1 red pepper, deseeded and chopped

2 Tbsp balti curry paste

1 tsp chilli powder or paste

200ml/7fl oz vegetable stock

225g/8oz tin chopped tomatoes

1 mango, peeled and flesh chopped

2 Tbsp chopped fresh coriander

Serves 4

1. Fill a wok one-third full with water and bring to the boil. Add the potatoes and carrots and cook for 5 minutes. Add the cauliflower florets and cook for a further 3 minutes, then drain. Carefully wipe the wok dry.

2. Heat the oil in the wok and fry the onion over a low heat for 5 minutes until softened. Add the courgette, red pepper, potatoes, carrots and cauliflower and fry for 3 minutes, stirring occasionally.

3. Stir in the curry paste and chilli, cook for 1 minute then pour in the stock and tomatoes. Lower the heat, cover and simmer for 15 minutes or until the vegetables are tender.

4. Stir in the mango and simmer for 2–3 minutes or until heated through. Serve sprinkled with the coriander.

Tagliatelle with caramelized onions and walnuts

375g/13oz tagliatelle

2 Tbsp olive oil, plus 1 tsp for the pasta

6 large red onions, finely sliced

2 garlic cloves, finely chopped

2 sprigs rosemary, chopped

1 small glass white wine

1 Tbsp walnut oil (optional)

125g/4oz walnuts, toasted and roughly chopped

110g/3½oz Gruyère cheese, grated

Serves 3–4

1. Heat a large pan of lightly salted water. When boiling, add the pasta and cook for 8–10 minutes. Drain, stir in 1 tsp olive oil and set aside.

2. Heat a large frying pan or wok over a medium heat, add the olive oil and cook the onions over a moderate heat for 15 minutes. Add the garlic and rosemary and cook for a further 2 minutes.

3. Pour in the wine and simmer until most of the wine has evaporated. Tip the pasta back into the red onion and toss well to mix everything. Stir in the walnut oil if using, followed by the walnuts and Gruyère.

Linguini with sweet onions and Swiss chard

2 Tbsp butter

2 Tbsp olive oil

2 large onions, peeled and finely sliced

500g/1lb 2oz linguini

1 Tbsp + tsp salt

1 bunch (about 300g/10oz) Swiss or rainbow chard

½ tsp freshly ground black pepper

125ml/4¼fl oz dry white wine

100g/4oz goat's cheese, crumbled

Serves 4

1. Heat the butter and olive oil in a pan over medium-high heat. Add the sliced onions and stir to coat the onions in the butter and oil. Cover the pan, reduce the heat to low, then leave the onions to slowly cook for 1 hour or until very soft. Uncover and continue cooking the onions until dark golden, about a further 25 minutes.

2. While the onions are cooking, prepare the chard. Cut 3cm/11/2in from the bottom of the stalks and discard. Slice the chard crosswise into 2cm/¾in wide slices.

3. Meanwhile, bring a large pan of water to the boil. Put the linguini in the pan, along with 1 Tbsp of salt and cook according to directions on packet.

4. Season the onions with salt and pepper, increase the heat, then add the wine. When the bubbles subside, add the chard. Stir well, turn the heat to medium-low, cover and stew until chard is wilted and tender, about 10 minutes.

5. Drain the pasta and toss with onion and chard mixture. Divide between four bowls and top with crumbled goat's cheese and add more salt and pepper to taste. Serve immediately.

Pumpkin ravioli with sage and pine nut butter

For the filling:

450g/1lb pumpkin or
  butternut squash, peeled,
  deseeded and chopped

1 tsp olive oil

30g/1¼oz Parmesan cheese,
  grated

Pinch freshly grated nutmeg

100g/4oz ricotta

Salt and freshly ground black
  pepper

1 quantity Egg pasta dough
  (see page 17)

For the butter:

100g/4oz butter

12–18 sage leaves

50g/2oz pine nuts, lightly
  toasted

Serves 4–6

1. Firstly prepare the filling. Preheat the oven to 200°C/400°F/Gas mark 6. Put the pumpkin in a roasting dish and drizzle with the oil. Toss to coat, then roast in the oven, stirring occasionally, for 25–30 minutes or until soft and tender. Remove from the oven and leave to cool slightly.

2. When cool enough to handle, mash the pumpkin using a fork. Add the Parmesan cheese, nutmeg and ricotta and mix well until smooth. Season generously with salt and pepper. Set aside.

3. Roll out the pasta to very thin – you should be able to see your fingers through it. Using a 5–6cm/2–2¼in round or fluted cutter, cut out 48–60 rounds, or as many as you can get out of the pasta. Using a teaspoon, put a small amount of the filling in the centre of half of the pasta rounds. Using your finger or a pastry brush, brush a little water around the edge of the disc and place a second disc on top, pressing the edges to seal. Use a fork to press the edges for a more decorative finish. As you go, set the ravioli aside on a floured tray until all are done.

4. Bring a large pan of cold water to the boil, reduce the water to a simmer then gently poach the ravioli for 4–5 minutes. Drain well.

5. Meanwhile prepare the butter. Heat the butter gently over a low heat with the sage leaves. Stir in the pine nuts then pour over the ravioli and serve immediately with black pepper.

Barley risotto with roasted butternut squash and goat's cheese

1 butternut squash or pumpkin (about 800g–1kg/1¾–2¼lb in weight)

1 red onion, peeled and cut into thin wedges

2 Tbsp olive oil

Salt

1 Tbsp butter

3 garlic cloves, peeled and crushed

250g/9oz pearl barley, rinsed

250ml/8fl oz white wine

1L/1¾pt hot vegetable stock

Small handful of flat-leaf parsley, chopped

75g/3oz goat's cheese, cut into small cubes

100g/4oz rocket or watercress, tough stalks removed

Freshly ground black pepper

Serves 4

1. Preheat the oven to 200°C/400°F/Gas mark 6. Peel and cut the squash into approximately 2cm/¾in cubes. Put the squash and red onion into a roasting pan and toss with 1 Tbsp of the oil. Season generously with salt and cook for 20–25 minutes, stirring once or twice until golden and cooked.

2. While the pumpkin is cooking prepare the remaining ingredients. Heat the remaining oil and the butter in a large, heavy-based saucepan and stir in the garlic and barley. Toss to coat in the oil and butter and stir for a couple of minutes. Add the wine, bring to the boil, and then simmer until the wine evaporates. Add a ladleful of hot stock. Each time the liquid evaporates add another ladleful of stock until it has all been added. Reduce the heat and simmer, stirring occasionally for 30–40 minutes. The barley should become tender while the mixture should remain slightly soupy.

3. Stir in the parsley, goat's cheese and half of the rocket, along with the pumpkin and red onion. Season to taste and serve with the remaining rocket on top.

Wild mushroom and parmesan risotto

5 Tbsp olive oil

500g/1lb 2 oz mixed
mushrooms (e.g. chestnut,
shiitake, oyster, porcini)
sliced or quartered
according to size

1 onion, peeled and finely
sliced

2 garlic cloves, peeled and
crushed

2 tsp chopped fresh oregano

Finely grated zest of ½ lemon

350g/12oz Arborio rice

150ml/¼ pt dry white wine

900ml/1½pt hot chicken or
vegetable stock

3 Tbsp grated Parmesan
cheese, plus extra for
shavings

2 Tbsp chopped fresh chives

Freshly ground black pepper

Serves 4

1. Heat 3 tablespoons of the oil in a wok and stir-fry the mushrooms over a medium heat for 5 minutes. Drain and set aside.

2. Add the rest of the oil to the wok, lower the heat and fry the onion and garlic for 5 minutes. Add the oregano, lemon zest and rice, stirring for 1–2 minutes until the grains are shiny.

3. Pour in the wine, bring to the boil and leave to bubble until the wine has nearly all evaporated. Add a ladleful of the hot stock and stir until it has been absorbed by the rice. Continue adding the stock, a ladleful at a time, allowing each lot to be absorbed before adding the next, until the rice is tender – this will take around 20 minutes.

4. Stir in the grated Parmesan cheese and then the mushrooms into the rice and scatter over the chives. Season with freshly ground black pepper and serve with Parmesan shavings scattered on top.

Roasted red onion, artichoke and sage calzone

2 red onions, peeled and cut into thin wedges

200g/7oz marinated artichokes, drained and quartered

12–16 sage leaves

1 tsp extra virgin olive oil

¼ quantity Crispy pizza base dough (see page 13)

100ml/3½fl oz Quick classic tomato sauce (see page 24)

30g/1¼oz finely grated Parmesan cheese

Chilli oil, to serve

Makes 2 long pizzas

1. Preheat the oven to 220°C/425°F/Gas mark 7. Put the onion, artichokes and sage leaves in a roasting tray with 1 tsp extra virgin olive oil. Cook for 15–20 minutes or until golden and starting to go crispy.

2. Divide the pizza dough into two balls. On a lightly floured surface roll each ball into an oblong shape about 25cm/10in long and 10cm/4in wide. Transfer the bases to a baking sheet ready to be topped and leave to rest.

3. Spread the tomato sauce evenly over the bases, leaving about a 1-cm/½-in border around the edge. Evenly scatter over the red onion wedges, artichoke quarters, sage leaves and Parmesan cheese. Cook in the middle of the preheated oven for 10–12 minutes or until golden and crispy. Serve immediately with chilli oil drizzled over.

Rocket and new potato focaccia

½ quantity Focaccia pizza base dough (see page 15)

4 Tbsp Rocket pesto (see page 20)

300g/10oz new potatoes, par-boiled for 8–10 minutes then sliced lengthways, about 5mm/¼in thick

40g/1½oz grated Gruyère cheese

Sea salt and freshly ground black pepper

50g/2oz rocket leaves

Chilli oil, to serve

Makes 1 pizza

1. On a lightly floured work surface roll out the dough into a rectangular shape about 30cm/12in long and 20cm/8in wide. Place on baking parchment or a baking sheet ready to be topped and leave to rest for 15–20 minutes. Preheat the oven to 220°C/425°F/Gas mark 7.

2. Make small indentations on the top of the dough using your fingertips. Spread the rocket pesto evenly over the base, leaving about a 1–2-cm/½–¾in border around the edges. Evenly place the potatoes over the pesto so they slightly overlap. Sprinkle over the Gruyère and season with salt and pepper. Cook in the middle of the preheated oven for about 14–16 minutes or until crisp and golden and the base is cooked through. Remove from the oven and throw over some fresh rocket leaves and a drizzle of chilli oil to serve.

Gorgonzola and roasted red onion pizza

2 large red onions

2 Tbsp olive oil

2 tsp caster sugar

Salt and pepper

1 x 30-cm/12-in Crispy pizza
base (see page 13)

250g/9oz Gorgonzola
cheese, crumbled

1 handful fresh flat-leaf
parsley, torn

Makes 1 pizza

1. Preheat the oven to 220°C/425°F/Gas mark 7. Peel the onions and cut each one into 8 wedges. Place them in a roasting tin and toss with olive oil, sugar and season with salt and pepper. Roast the onions for 30–40 minutes, stirring every 10 minutes, until caramelized. Remove from the heat and leave the oven on at the same temperature.

2. Prepare the pizza base so it is ready to be topped. Top the base with Gorgonzola and roasted red onions leaving a 1–2cm/½–¾in border around the edge. Bake for 10–12 minutes, or until the cheese has melted and the crust is golden. Sprinkle with parsley and serve immediately.

Walnut pesto, aubergine and pomegranate pizza

1 x 30cm/12in Crispy pizza base (see page 13)

3 Tbsp Walnut pesto (see page 20)

350g/12oz aubergine, cut into 2cm/¾in cubes

2 Tbsp extra virgin olive oil

60g/2¼oz crumbled feta cheese

2 Tbsp pomegranate seeds

For the vinaigrette:

2 Tbsp olive oil

1 Tbsp pomegranate molasses

1 tsp runny honey

¼ tsp cumin seeds, lightly crushed

Makes 1 pizza

1. Prepare the pizza base so it is ready to be topped. Preheat the oven to 220°C/425°F/Gas mark 7.

2. Prepare the Walnut pesto and set aside. Put the aubergine cubes in a roasting pan and toss with olive oil. Roast for 20 minutes, until slightly wilted and discoloured. Remove from the heat and keep the oven on at the same temperature. Toss the vinaigrette ingredients in a medium-sized bowl and add the roasted aubergine cubes, tossing to coat.

3. Spread the Walnut pesto over the base leaving a 1–2cm/½–¾in border around the edge. Spoon the aubergine cubes over the pesto and top with feta. Bake in the middle of the oven for 10–12 minutes, until the crust is golden. Remove from the oven, garnish with pomegranate seeds and serve immediately.

Black bean and vegetable chilli with coriander-lime crème fraîche

For the chilli:

4 Tbsp olive oil

2 onions, peeled and roughly chopped

2 red peppers, cored, deseeded and roughly chopped

3 garlic cloves, peeled and finely chopped

2 chipotle chillies in adobo sauce, roughly chopped

1 Tbsp ground cumin

1 Tbsp ground coriander

2 tsp chilli powder

2 x 425g/15oz tins black beans, drained and rinsed

2 x 425g/15oz tins crushed tomatoes

75ml/2½ fl oz runny honey

75ml/2½ fl oz cider vinegar

300g/10oz frozen sweetcorn

250–500ml/8–18fl oz vegetable stock, depending on desired thickness

For the crème fraîche:

200ml/7fl oz crème fraîche or soured cream

3 Tbsp finely chopped fresh coriander

Zest and juice of 1 lime

Serves 4–6

1. Heat the olive oil in a large soup pot over medium-high heat. Add the onions, peppers, garlic and chillies and cook, stirring occasionally, until beginning to soften, about 5 minutes. Add the cumin, ground coriander and chilli powder and stir for 1 minute more. Add the beans, tomatoes, honey, cider vinegar, sweetcorn and enough stock just to cover. Simmer over a low heat for 15 minutes, stirring occasionally.

2. Combine the crème fraîche, fresh coriander, and the lime juice and zest in a small bowl.

3. To serve, divide the chilli between 4–6 warmed bowls, and top with a dollop of the crème fraîche.

Beef tomatoes stuffed with cheese & spinach

4 firm beef or marmade tomatoes, about 9cm/3½ inches in diameter

4 Tbsp grated Gruyère or mozzarella cheese

For the stuffing:

225g/8oz cooked fresh, frozen or tinned spinach, well drained

2 cloves garlic, finely chopped

2 Tbsp finely chopped spring onions

120g/4½ oz paneer, crumbled

1 Tbsp finely chopped fresh coriander

1 Tbsp chopped fresh mint

1 or 2 green chillies, finely chopped

1 tsp garam masala

1 tsp cumin seeds

1 tsp mustard seeds

½ tsp mango powder

1 tsp salt

Makes 4

1. Mix the stuffing ingredients together until the stuffing is soft and mouldable and set aside.

2. Cut the top off each tomato and discard. Without making a hole in the sides of the tomatoes, carefully scoop out and discard the seeds and central pulp.

3. Spoon the stuffing mixture into the tomato cavities and place them on a sheet of foil on an oven tray. Top each tomato with 1 tablespoon cheese then bake in a preheated oven, 160°C/325°F/Gas Mark 3, for 15–20 minutes. Serve hot.

Mushroom, wild rice and ale pie

200g/7oz Portobello
mushrooms

200g/7oz chestnut
mushrooms

200g/7oz wild mushrooms
(e.g. shiitake, enoki,
chanterelle)

30g/1¼oz butter

2 Tbsp olive oil

1 onion, peeled and finely
chopped

30g/1¼oz dried porcini,
soaked in 200ml/7fl oz
boiling water

3 garlic cloves, peeled and
crushed

250g/8oz celeriac, peeled
and cut into 1cm/½in cubes

2 Tbsp plain flour

150ml/5fl oz dark ale

100g/4oz freshly-cooked
wild rice

Salt and freshly ground black
pepper

500g/1lb 2oz puff pastry

2 Tbsp chopped fresh thyme
leaves or flat-leaf parsley

Milk to glaze

Serves 4–6

1. Rinse the mushrooms and wipe clean. Cut each
Portobello mushroom into eight, the chestnut mushrooms in
half and the rest as appropriate.

2. Heat the butter and oil in a large heavy-based
saucepan and sauté the onion until soft and translucent
but not brown. Drain the porcini, reserving the liquid and
chop finely. Add the garlic and chopped porcini to the
pan and sauté for 1 minute before adding the celeriac.
Stir to coat in the oil then add the mushrooms. Keep the
heat high and cook the mushrooms until softened.

3. Gradually add the flour and stir gently until evenly
combined. Add the ale and reserved porcini liquid and
stir, over a high heat, until the sauce thickens before
stirring in the rice. Season to taste. Continue to cook for a
further 2–3 minutes then remove from the heat and cool
to room temperature.

4. Preheat the oven to 220°C/425°F/Gas mark 7. Roll
out two-thirds of the pastry on a lightly-floured surface to
3–4mm/⅛in thick and use to line a 23cm/9in rimmed pie
tin. Stir the thyme or parsley into the mushroom mixture then
spoon into the pie tin. Brush the rim of the pastry with milk.

5. Roll out the remaining pastry and lie it over the top of
the mushroom mixture and trim to fit. Using your fingers or
a fork, pinch the pie edge together. Make a cross in the
centre of the pie and brush with a little more milk. Cook
in the oven for 40–50 minutes or until golden and crispy.
Serve immediately.

Herbed potato pie

5 large baking potatoes, peeled

2 cloves garlic, peeled and crushed

3 shallots, peeled and sliced

2 Tbsp freshly chopped herbs (parsley, chives, rosemary, thyme)

125g/4½oz Cheddar cheese, grated

50g/1¾oz Parmesan cheese, grated

425ml/15fl oz vegetable stock

Serves 4

1. Preheat the oven to 180°C/350°F/Gas Mark 4. Slice the potatoes very thinly. Butter an ovenproof dish and layer one third of the potatoes in the dish. Sprinkle over one third of the garlic, shallots, herbs and grated Cheddar cheese.

2. Repeat the layers two more times until all the ingredients are used.

3. Sprinkle the top with grated Parmesan cheese and pour over the hot stock. Bake in the oven for 30–40 minutes or until the potatoes are soft and the cheese is golden.

Leek, fennel and basil tart

375g/13oz shortcrust pastry

2 Tbsp extra-virgin olive oil

30g/1oz butter

1 onion, peeled and finely chopped

1 fennel bulb, finely diced

350g/12oz leeks, thinly sliced

1 garlic clove, peeled and crushed

150g/5oz mascarpone

75ml/2fl oz double cream

4 large eggs, beaten

50g/2oz Parmesan cheese, grated

Large handful of fresh basil leaves, roughly torn

Salt and freshly ground black pepper

Serves 6

1. On a lightly-floured surface, roll out the pastry to 3–4mm/⅛in thick and use to line a 28cm/10in loose-bottomed tart tin. Chill the pastry for about 20 minutes. Preheat the oven to 200°C/400°F/Gas Mark 6.

2. When the pastry has chilled, line it with baking paper and baking beans and bake for 15 minutes. Remove the baking paper and beans and return to the oven for a further 5 minutes or until lightly golden.

3. Meanwhile prepare the filling. In a large heavy-based saucepan heat the oil and butter. Add the onion, fennel and leeks and sweat until cooked and tender but not browned, about 6–8 minutes. Stir in the garlic and cook for a further minute then remove from the heat.

4. In a separate bowl combine the mascarpone, cream and eggs and lightly beat together. Add the cream mixture, Parmesan cheese and basil leaves to the leek mixture and stir to combine. Season generously with salt and pepper.

5. Reduce oven temperature to 180°C/350°F/Gas Mark 4. Pour the filling mixture into the warm pastry case and bake in the oven for 25–35 minutes or until set and golden on top. Serve warm or at room temperature.

Spicy sweetcorn patties

75g/3oz fine green beans, finely chopped

½ red pepper, deseeded and finely chopped

4 spring onions, finely chopped

100g/4oz sweetcorn kernels

1 Tbsp Thai red curry paste

1 Tbsp light soy sauce

1 tsp brown sugar

1 Tbsp chopped fresh parsley

75g/3oz plain flour

1 egg, beaten

Vegetable oil for frying

To garnish:
Shredded spring onions
Fine slices of red chilli
Fresh parsley sprigs

Serves 4

1. Place the green beans, red pepper and spring onions in a bowl with the sweetcorn and stir in the curry paste, soy sauce, sugar and chopped parsley.

2. Add the flour and stir until all the vegetables are coated, then beat in the egg so the ingredients bind together.

3. Heat 2.5cm/1in of oil in a wok and carefully drop dessertspoonfuls of the mixture into the hot oil. Fry in batches for 3–4 minutes until the patties are golden brown. Drain on a plate lined with absorbent kitchen paper and serve hot garnished with shredded spring onions, fine slices of red chilli and parsley sprigs.

Root vegetable and winter herb cakes

225g/8oz sweet potatoes

225g/8oz potatoes

Sunflower oil for frying

1 onion, peeled and finely chopped

225g/8oz carrots, peeled and grated

2 tsp fresh thyme leaves

2 tsp chopped fresh rosemary

Plain flour, to dust

1 egg, beaten

50g/2oz fresh breadcrumbs

Serves 4

1. Scrub the unpeeled sweet potatoes and ordinary potatoes and cook in a pan of boiling water (this can be done in the wok) until tender when pierced with a skewer. Drain and, when the potatoes are cool enough to handle, peel, place in a bowl and coarsely crush with a fork. (Carefully dry the wok if you have used it to cook the potatoes.)

2. Heat 2 tablespoons of oil in the wok and fry the onion over a low heat for 5 minutes. Stir in the carrots, thyme and rosemary and cook for 2 minutes. Add to the crushed potatoes and stir until mixed.

3. Leave to cool and then shape the mixture into 8 round flat cakes. Dust with flour, brush with beaten egg and coat in the breadcrumbs. Chill for about 1 hour to firm up.

4. Heat 2.5cm/1in of oil in the wok and fry the cakes in two batches. Fry each batch for about 5 minutes, until golden brown on both sides, turning over halfway through cooking. Drain on a plate lined with absorbent kitchen paper and serve hot.

Chickpea and coriander cakes

200g/7oz tinned chickpeas, drained and rinsed

150g/5oz freshly-cooked brown rice

50g/2oz oatmeal, uncooked

1 tsp coriander seeds

1 tsp cumin seeds

3 Tbsp groundnut or vegetable oil

1 small onion, peeled and finely chopped

1 celery stick, finely chopped

2 garlic cloves, peeled and minced

1 small red chilli, deseeded and finely chopped

20g/¾oz fresh coriander, tops and roots separated, roots chopped

1 tsp turmeric

1 Tbsp flaky salt

zest and juice of 1 lemon

3 Tbsp Greek yogurt, crème fraîche or soured cream

Rhubarb chutney, to serve (optional)

Makes 8

1. Combine chickpeas, rice and oatmeal in a large bowl and set aside. Toast the coriander and cumin seeds in a dry frying pan over medium-high heat until the seeds are fragrant and begin to pop. Transfer to a pestle and mortar and grind until smooth.

2. Heat 1 Tbsp of oil in a frying pan over medium heat. Add the onion, celery, garlic, chilli and chopped coriander roots and sauté until soft, about 10 minutes. Stir in ground coriander, cumin seed and turmeric. Transfer the mixture to the bowl with the chickpeas, rice and oatmeal. Stir in the salt, lemon zest and juice, Greek yogurt and coriander leaves. Place the mixture in a food processor and pulse until almost smooth.

3. Form the mixture into cakes – make either 8 or 12, depending on whether you are serving them as a starter or main course. Heat 2 Tbsp oil in a nonstick frying pan and heat until very hot. Fry the cakes for 3–4 minutes each side, or until browned. Serve immediately, with rhubarb chutney, if liked.

Spinach crêpes with mixed mushrooms

250g/8oz spinach, trimmed

1 quantity Basic crêpe batter (see page 25), unsweetened

2 tsp olive oil

2 shallots, finely chopped

2 cloves garlic, finely chopped

60g/2oz unsalted butter

1 Tbsp finely chopped fresh thyme

350g/12oz assorted mushrooms e.g. button, oyster, chestnut, shiitake, wiped and sliced

4 Tbsp dry white wine

300ml/10fl oz double cream

Salt and black pepper

Fresh thyme, to garnish

Serves 4

1. Wash the spinach and pack into a saucepan whilst still wet. Cover the pan with a lid and cook the spinach over gentle heat for about 5 minutes, until the leaves are wilted. Drain well, pressing against the sides of a colander to extract as much water as possible. Allow to cool and then chop finely.

2. Prepare the batter and stir in the chopped spinach. Make the crêpes and keep warm. Take care not to over-cook them as they will be thicker and more difficult to fold.

3. Heat the oil in a large frying pan and gently fry the shallots and garlic for 3 minutes, until just softened. Add the butter and melt until bubbling, then stir in the thyme and mushrooms and cook, stirring, for about 5 minutes until browned and tender.

4. Stir in the wine and cream and bring to a simmer, and heat through for about 3 minutes, until piping hot. Season, then fill the crêpes with the mushroom mixture. Garnish with thyme.

Poppy seed waffles with ratatouille

1 aubergine

Salt

1 quantity Basic waffle batter (see page 27), unsweetened and made with gluten-free flour, gluten-free baking powder, soya milk and vegan margarine

2 Tbsp poppy seeds

2 Tbsp olive oil

1 tsp coriander seeds, crushed

1 large onion, chopped

1 clove garlic, crushed

1 large red pepper, deseeded and chopped

1 large courgette, trimmed and chopped

2 bay leaves

400g/14oz tin chopped tomatoes

4 Tbsp dry red wine

2 Tbsp tomato purée

1 tsp caster sugar

Freshly ground black pepper

2 Tbsp finely chopped fresh parsley

Serves 4

1. Trim the aubergine and cut into small pieces. Layer up in a colander or strainer, sprinkling with salt as you go, and allow to stand for 30 minutes. Rinse well and pat dry with absorbent kitchen paper.

2. Meanwhile, make up the waffle batter. Stir in the poppy seeds and cook as directed to make about 10 waffles. Keep warm.

3. Heat the oil in a large saucepan and gently fry the coriander seeds, onion, garlic and pepper for 5 minutes. Stir in the aubergine and cook for a further 3 minutes. Add the remaining ingredients, except the parsley, mix well and bring to the boil. Cover and simmer for about 20 minutes, until just tender. Serve the sauce piled on top of the waffles and sprinkle with parsley.

Greek salad

3 Tbsp olive oil

1 Tbsp lemon juice

1 tsp dried oregano

Pinch of salt and freshly
ground black pepper

4 tomatoes, sliced

1 onion, peeled and thinly
sliced

1 cucumber, diced

125g/4oz feta cheese,
cubed

16 olives

Serves 4

1. In a small bowl, mix together the olive oil, lemon juice, oregano, salt and pepper, and set aside.

2. In a separate bowl, mix together the tomatoes, onion, cucumber, feta and olives. Transfer to a serving bowl and pour the olive oil mixture over the salad and toss well.

Desserts

Dark chocolate ice cream

4 large egg yolks

125g/4oz plus 2 Tbsp caster sugar

500ml/16fl oz full-cream milk

100g/3½oz plain chocolate (70% cocoa solids) broken into pieces

45g/1½oz cocoa powder

Makes 600ml/1 pt

1. In a heatproof bowl beat (using an electric whisk) the egg yolks with 125g/4oz sugar until thick and creamy. Gently heat the milk in a saucepan to near-boiling point, then pour into the bowl of egg mixture, beating well.

2. Melt the chocolate in a heatproof bowl over a pan of simmering water. Beat the melted chocolate into the egg mixture, followed by the cocoa. Place the bowl over a pan of simmering water and stir with a wooden spoon until the bubbles deflate and the mixture coats the back of the spoon. Remove from the heat. Meanwhile, in a very small saucepan, make a caramel by combining 2 tablespoons of sugar with 2 tablespoons of water. Boil the mixture until it turns dark amber in colour, swirling the pan as it begins to darken. When it reaches 180°C/350°F on a sugar thermometer, it is ready.

3. Whisk the caramel into the chocolate until smooth – it will sizzle. Cover the surface with clingfilm and cool. Leave in the fridge for at least 1 hour, then churn in an ice cream maker, according to the manufacturer's instructions. Serve or transfer to a freezer container, cover the surface with greaseproof paper or foil and put in the freezer.

Blueberry cheesecake ice cream

175ml/6fl oz full-fat milk

3 large egg yolks

150g/5oz caster sugar

300g/10oz cream cheese

100g/3½oz white chocolate, melted

250g/8oz Blueberry compôte (see page 28)

Makes 600ml/1pt

1. Heat the milk gently to near-boiling point. In a separate heatproof bowl, beat the egg yolks and sugar, using an electric whisk, until thick and pale. Place over a pan of simmering water and slowly add the milk, stirring constantly. Stir occasionally until the mixture is thick enough to coat the back of a wooden spoon. Remove from the heat and cool for 20 minutes.

2. Beat in the cream cheese, using an electric whisk, until smooth. Stir in the cooled, melted white chocolate and the blueberry compôte until just combined then transfer to a freezer container. Cover the surface directly with greaseproof paper or foil and put in the freezer. After 1 hour of freezing stir the mixture to prevent the berries from sinking to the bottom and return to the freezer for a further 4 hours or overnight. Serve with extra blueberry compôte drizzled over the top if liked.

Traditional rocky road ice cream

1 quantity Milk chocolate ice cream (see below) using 150g/5oz milk chocolate (instead of 100g/3½oz milk chocolate) and 50g/1¾oz plain chocolate, unchurned

60g/2oz whole almonds, toasted and chopped

60g/2oz mini marshmallows

60g/2oz digestive biscuits, broken

60g/2oz soft jelly sweets, chopped if large

For the milk chocolate ice cream:

250ml/8fl oz full-cream milk

2 large egg yolks

50g/1¾oz caster sugar

150g/5oz good-quality milk chocolate, broken into pieces

50g/1¾oz plain chocolate (70% cocoa solids), broken into pieces

150ml/5fl oz double cream

Makes 600ml/1pt

1. Place the milk in a medium saucepan and heat gently to near-boiling point. Beat the egg yolks and sugar in a heatproof bowl, using an electric whisk, until thick and pale. Gradually beat the milk into the egg mixture.

2. Place the bowl over a pan of simmering water and continue stirring until the mixture is thick enough to coat the back of a wooden spoon. Remove the bowl from the heat and stir in chocolate pieces, stirring until smooth. Cover the surface directly with clingfilm or greaseproof paper to prevent a skin forming. Allow the custard to cool completely.

3. Once cool, stir in the cream and churn in an ice cream maker according to the manufacturer's instructions. Stir in the remaining ingredients and transfer to a freezer container with a lid or gently cover with greaseproof paper or foil and put in the freezer.

Passionfruit sorbet

20 passionfruit, flesh
  scooped out
600ml/1pt water
200g/7oz caster sugar
Juice of 2 limes

Makes 600ml/1pt

1. Place the passionfruit flesh, water, sugar and lime juice in a large saucepan. Stir until the sugar has dissolved. Bring to the boil then reduce the heat and simmer for 5 minutes. Cool the syrup completely.

2. Churn in an ice cream maker, according to the manufacturer's instructions, until frozen. Serve immediately or transfer to a freezer container, cover the surface directly with greaseproof paper or foil and put in the freezer.

3. Remove from the freezer 15 minutes before serving to allow it to soften slightly.

Tiramisu ice cream torta

100g/3½oz caster sugar

300ml/10fl oz water

1 Tbsp instant coffee powder
150g/5oz amaretti biscuits
or sponge fingers

45ml/1½fl oz Tia Maria,
marsala or dark rum

250ml/8fl oz double cream

200g/7oz mascarpone

Makes 900ml/1½pt

1. Line the base and sides of a loaf tin (23 x 12 x 6cm/ 9 x 4¾ x 2⅓in) with greaseproof paper or foil and set aside.

2. Put the sugar, water and coffee powder in a saucepan and bring to the boil, stirring constantly. Simmer for 5 minutes, uncovered, then cool completely. Soak the amaretti biscuits in the alcohol.

3. Whip the cream until stiff peaks form then add the mascarpone and beat until combined. Slowly stir the coffee syrup mixture into the cream and continue beating until smooth.

4. Use a third of the soaked biscuits to line the base of the tin. Roughly crush the remaining biscuits and fold through the coffee-cream mixture. Pour the coffee-cream mixture over the amaretti. Cover the surface directly with greaseproof paper or foil and put in the freezer. To serve, remove the torta from the tin and cut into slices. Serve sprinkled with cocoa powder, if liked.

White chocolate and berry pie

150g/5oz butter

250g/8oz shortbread fingers, crushed

250g/8oz white chocolate

300ml/10fl oz soured cream

2 Tbsp dark rum (optional)

300ml/10fl oz double cream

250g/8oz prepared, assorted summer berries

White chocolate decorations, to finish

Serves 8–10

1. Grease and line the base and sides of a 20cm/8in spring-release cake tin. Melt 90g/3oz of the butter in a saucepan, remove from the heat and then mix in the crushed shortbread. Press into the base of the tin. Chill until required.

2. Break the chocolate into pieces and place in a small heatproof bowl. Add the remaining butter and stand the bowl over a pan of gently simmering water. Allow to melt, then remove from the water and stir in the sour cream and rum if using.

3. Whip the double cream to form soft peaks and fold into the chocolate cream. Spoon over the biscuit base and smooth the top. Chill for at least 6 hours or overnight.

4. When ready to serve, remove from the tin and place on a serving plate. Top with the berries and finish off with shavings of white chocolate. Cut into slices to serve.

Chocolate banoffee pie

90g/3oz butter

250g/8oz double chocolate chip cookies, crushed

3 ripe medium-sized bananas

397g/14oz tin condensed milk

1 Tbsp cocoa powder

300ml/10fl oz double cream

Grated milk chocolate, to decorate

Serves 6

1. Grease the bases and sides of six individual 8cm/3in loose-bottomed cake tins or cake rings. Melt the butter in a saucepan, then remove from the heat. Mix the crushed cookies with the melted butter and divide between the six tins. Press firmly into the base of each. Slice the bananas thinly and arrange over the biscuit base. Cover and chill until required.

2. Pour the condensed milk into a saucepan, bring to the boil and simmer over a medium heat, stirring, until the milk turns a toffee colour. Remove from the heat, sieve over the cocoa and add 6 Tbsp double cream and mix well. Spoon the toffee filling over the bananas and biscuit base. Cover and chill for 30 minutes.

3. When ready to serve, remove the pies from the tins and place on serving plates. Whip the remaining double cream and pile on top of each one. Sprinkle with grated chocolate and serve.

Poached rhubarb with ginger cake

For the ginger cake:

60g/2oz treacle

60g/2oz golden syrup

60g/2oz dark brown sugar

60g/2oz unsalted butter

75ml/2½fl oz full-fat milk

125g/4oz self-raising flour

½ tsp salt

½ tsp ground ginger

½ tsp ground cinnamon

30g/1oz stem ginger in syrup, finely chopped

For the rhubarb:

350g/12oz rhubarb

125g/4oz caster sugar

125ml/4fl oz freshly squeezed orange juice

Serves 4

1. Preheat the oven to 170°C/325°F/Gas mark 3. Grease and line a 500g/1lb loaf tin. Place the treacle, syrup, sugar, butter and milk in a saucepan, and heat gently, stirring, until melted together. Sift the flour, salt and spices in a bowl, and make a well in the centre. Add the ginger and gradually stir in the melted ingredients until well mixed. Transfer to the prepared tin and bake in the centre of the oven for about 55 minutes until risen and firm to the touch. Leave to cool in the tin, then remove from the tin, wrap in greaseproof paper and then foil, and store for 24 hours.

2. Trim and cut the rhubarb into 10cm/4in lengths. Place the sugar in a medium frying pan with a lid and pour in the orange juice. Heat gently, stirring until dissolved, then bring to the boil and simmer for 3 minutes.

3. Add the rhubarb to the pan, laying the pieces side by side. Bring back to the boil, cover and simmer for 3 minutes. Carefully turn the rhubarb over, cover and cook for a further 3–4 minutes until just cooked. Remove from the heat and allow to cool completely. Transfer to a serving dish, cover and chill for 2 hours before serving. To serve, slice the cake into 8 pieces. Place two slices on each serving plate and spoon over rhubarb and juices.

Deep-dish apple pie

2 quantities pastry (see Fresh
   lime tart recipe, page 275)
   or 750g/1½lb ready-made
   shortcrust pastry

1kg/2lb cooking apples

Finely grated rind and juice
   of 1 large lemon

125g/4oz light brown sugar

2 Tbsp cornflour

1½ tsp ground mixed spice

60g/2oz sultanas

30g/1oz unsalted butter

1 egg white, beaten

1 Tbsp caster sugar

To serve:

Custard sauce (see page 29)
ice cream or pouring cream

Serves 6 to 8

1. Preheat the oven to 190°C/375°F/Gas mark 5. Make up the pastry as directed on page 275. Roll out two thirds of the pastry on a lightly floured surface and use to line a 23cm/9in round spring-release cake tin. Chill for 30 minutes.

2. Meanwhile, peel, core and thinly slice the apples. Place in a bowl and toss in the lemon rind and juice. In another bowl, mix the brown sugar, cornflour and mixed spice together.

3. Sprinkle a little of the sugar mixture over the base of the pastry case, and mix the remainder into the apples together with the sultanas. Pack down into the pastry case and dot the top with the butter.

4. Roll out the remaining pastry to fit the top of the pie. Brush the pie edge with a little egg white and press the pie lid on top. Trim and seal the edges. Using a sharp knife, make a small hole in the centre of the pie lid so that the steam can escape. Place a baking sheet in the oven for 5 minutes.

5. Brush the top of the pie with egg white and sprinkle with caster sugar. Stand the tin on the hot baking sheet and bake for 45–50 minutes until the apple is tender – push a skewer into the centre to see if it is cooked – and the top is golden. Stand for 10 minutes before unclipping the tin. Serve the pie hot or cold, with custard, ice cream or pouring cream.

Raspberry cheesecake

350g/12oz double chocolate chip cookies, crushed

125g/4oz unsalted butter

250g/8oz white chocolate, broken into pieces

300g/10oz full-fat soft cheese, at room temperature

250ml/8fl oz double cream, at room temperature

1 tsp vanilla extract

250g/8oz fresh raspberries plus extra to decorate (optional)

Serves 10

1. Grease and line the base of a deep 23cm/9in spring-release cake tin. Place the cookies in a bowl. Melt the butter, pour over the cookies and bind together. Press on to the base of the tin using the back of a metal spoon. Chill until required.

2. Place the chocolate pieces in a heatproof bowl and melt over a pan of barely simmering water, and set aside for 10 minutes until it is cooled, but still warm. In a large mixing bowl, whisk together the cream cheese, double cream and vanilla extract.

3. Fold in the warm white chocolate and raspberries and spoon the mixture over the biscuit base. Smooth the top and chill for 2–3 hours until set. Note: if the chocolate is too cool, it will not mix in properly and will make the cheese filling lumpy. To serve, release the cheesecake from the tin and place on a serving plate. Top with extra raspberries if liked.

Pear and ginger cheesecake

60g/2oz unsalted butter

180g/6oz ginger biscuits, crushed

250g/8oz full-fat soft cheese

250g/8oz mascarpone

Finely grated rind of 1 lemon

1 Tbsp lemon juice

2 eggs, beaten

125g/4oz caster sugar

350g/12oz ripe pears, peeled, cored and thinly sliced

To serve:

Pouring cream

Fruit coulis (see page 28)

Serves 8

1. Preheat the oven to 150°C/300°F/Gas mark 2. Grease and line a 20cm/8in spring-release cake tin. Melt the butter in a saucepan. Remove from the heat and stir in the crushed biscuits. Press the mixture into the base of the tin using the back of a spoon. Chill until required.

2. In a mixing bowl, beat the soft cheese and mascarpone together until soft. Stir in the lemon rind and juice, and whisk in the eggs and sugar. Gently stir in the pears until well mixed.

3. Transfer to the tin and stand on a baking sheet. Bake for about 1½ hours, covering the top lightly with foil if it begins to brown too quickly, until firm and set. Turn off the heat, leave the oven door ajar, and allow the cheesecake to cool in the oven.

4. Carefully remove from the tin, transfer to a serving plate and chill for 2 hours before serving. Serve with pouring cream and Fruit coulis (see page 28).

Melon and mint tea salad

½ quantity Sugar syrup,
without the cocoa powder
 (see page 29)

1 tsp Indian tea leaves

150ml (5fl oz) boiling water

1 small bunch mint,
 plus extra to serve

½ small green-fleshed melon,
 e.g. Galia

½ small orange-fleshed
melon, e.g. Cantaloupe

¼ Honeydew melon

Serves 4

1. First make the syrup as directed on page 29 and allow to cool. Place the tea leaves in a heatproof jug and pour over the boiling water. Allow to brew for 3 minutes, then strain into another jug and put the small bunch of mint leaves into the tea. Allow to cool.

2. Scoop the seeds out of the melon. Slice off the skin and chop the flesh into small pieces and place in a serving bowl. Cover and chill until required.

3. Once the syrup and tea are cold, discard the mint leaves and mix the syrup and tea together. Pour over the melon, mix well, cover and chill for 30 minutes. Mix again before serving, sprinkled with extra mint leaves.

Mango pudding

For the milk pudding:

250ml/9fl oz milk

3 Tbsp cornflour

75ml/3fl oz water

50g/2oz caster sugar

2 tsp rose water

For the mango layer:

500ml/17fl oz mango juice

3 Tbsp cornflour

75ml/3fl oz water

50g/2oz caster sugar

Whipped cream (optional),
 to garnish

3 Tbsp ground pistachio nuts,
 to garnish

Serves 5

1. Start by making the milk pudding. Place the milk in a heavy-based saucepan. In a bowl, dissolve the cornflour in the water and add to the milk. Bring to the boil, reduce the heat and simmer gently for 15 minutes, until the mixture starts to thicken. Add the sugar and rose water and simmer for a further 5 minutes, stirring frequently. Remove from the heat and set aside.

2. To make the mango layer, place the mango juice in a saucepan. In a bowl, dissolve the cornflour in the water and add to the mango juice. Bring to the boil, reduce the heat and simmer gently for 15 minutes, until the mixture starts to thicken. Add the sugar and simmer for a further 5 minutes, stirring frequently. Remove from the heat.

3. Half fill five serving bowls with the milk pudding. Top with the mango syrup and garnish with whipped cream, if using, and sprinkle with ground pistachios.

Fresh lime tart

For the pastry:

180g/6oz plain flour

1 pinch salt

90g/3oz caster sugar

90g/3oz unsalted butter

1 egg yolk

Few drops vanilla extract

For the filling:

4 limes, scrubbed

115g/4oz + 1 Tbsp caster
sugar

3 eggs, beaten

60g/2oz unsalted butter,
melted

To serve:

Fruit coulis (see page 28)

Serves 6

1. Preheat the oven to 200°C/400°F/Gas mark 6. For the pastry, sift the flour, salt and sugar into a bowl, and rub in the butter to form a mixture that resembles fresh breadcrumbs. Mix in the egg yolk and vanilla essence and bring the mixture together, then knead gently to form a firm dough. Wrap and chill for 30 minutes.

2. Meanwhile, make the filling. Using a vegetable peeler, pare off a few strips of zest from one of the limes, and cut into thin shreds. Simmer in a little water for about 5 minutes until tender. Drain well and pat dry with absorbent kitchen paper. Toss in 1 Tbsp sugar then set aside in a warm place to dry.

3. Grate the rind from the remaining limes and extract the juice from all of them. Beat the rind, juice, sugar and eggs together. Cover and chill until required.

4. Roll out the pastry on a lightly floured surface to fit a 23cm/9in fluted loose-bottomed flan tin. The pastry is very short so you may find it easier to mould the pastry into the tin. Prick the base all over with a fork and bake in the oven for 12–15 minutes until lightly golden. Reduce the oven temperature to 180°C/350°F/Gas mark 4.

5. Whisk the melted butter into the lime filling and then pour into the pastry case. Bake in the oven for a further 20 minutes until just set. Allow to cool in the tin, then remove from the tin and chill until required. To serve, top the lime tart with the shredded lime zest. Serve with a Berry coulis (see page 28).

Almond and grape pastry

200g/7oz ground almonds

125g/4oz caster sugar

Seeds from 4 green
cardamom pods, crushed

1 tsp good-quality vanilla
extract

2 eggs, beaten

200g/7oz puff pastry,
defrosted if frozen

200g/7oz small seedless red
grapes, washed

60g/2oz flaked almonds

1 Tbsp icing sugar

To serve:

Pouring cream

Serves 8

1. Preheat the oven to 200°C/400°F/Gas mark 6. Line a baking tray with baking parchment.

2. Mix together the ground almonds, caster sugar, cardamom and vanilla. Bind together with one of the eggs to form a thick paste. Set aside.

3. Roll out the pastry on a lightly floured board to form a rectangle about 35 x 25cm/14 x 10in. Roll or press the almond paste to form a thick strip about 7cm/3in wide, and position it down the centre of the pastry, about 2.5cm/1in away from either end. Pile the grapes on top, gently pressing them into the almond paste.

4. Brush the edges of the pastry with beaten egg and fold up the two shorter sides, and then the longer sides to cover the filling completely. Press the top down lightly to seal. Transfer to the baking sheet and brush with more egg. Sprinkle with the almonds and bake in the oven for 35–40 minutes until golden and crisp. Cool on the baking tray then dust with icing sugar before slicing to serve. Best served warm, with pouring cream.

Filo stuffed with nuts

For the pastry:

500g/1lb 2 oz (22 sheets) filo pastry

200g/7oz unsalted butter, melted

For the nut filling:

250g/9oz coarsely ground almonds, walnuts or pine nuts

100g/3½oz caster sugar

1 tsp orange flower water

For the sugar syrup:

400g/14oz caster sugar

375ml/12½fl oz water

1 tsp lemon juice

2 tsp orange flower water

Makes about 40 pieces

1. Allow the filo pastry to reach room temperature before using. Brush a large baking dish with a little melted butter. Trim the edges of the filo pastry to fit the size of the dish. Place a sheet of filo in the baking dish. Brush it with butter and top with another sheet, keeping the remainder covered with a damp towel. Repeat in the same manner until half (approximately 10) of the filo sheets are used.

2. Preheat the oven to 190°C/375°F. To make the filling, combine the nuts with the sugar and orange flower water. Spread the nut filling over the filo sheets in the baking dish. Place a sheet of filo over the filling, brush with butter and repeat in the same manner until all sheets are used. Brush the top layer with butter and cut the layers into diamond shapes with a sharp knife. Bake for 1 hour until the top is lightly coloured. Drain any excess fat.

3. In the meantime, make the sugar syrup. Add the sugar and water to a saucepan, stirring over a medium heat until dissolved. Simmer for 15 minutes without stirring, then stir in the lemon juice and orange flower water just before removing from heat. When the syrup has cooled, pour it over the hot pastry and set aside to cool. Cut the pastry and store at room temperature in an air-tight container.

Apple, sultana and cinnamon strudel

½ quantity Sweet honey pizza base dough (see page 16)

2–3 (about 500g/1lb 2oz) apples, peeled, cored and sliced

Juice of 1 lemon

4 Tbsp sultanas

2 Tbsp brandy

1 tsp cinnamon

½ tsp ground nutmeg

2 Tbsp caster sugar (optional)

2 Tbsp melted butter

2 Tbsp brown sugar

Pouring cream, to serve

Makes 2 pizza strudels

1. Preheat the oven to 220°C/425°F/Gas mark 7. Divide the dough into two and roll each out into 30cm/12in rounds, on baking parchment, and leave to rest for about 10 minutes.

2. In a bowl combine the apple slices, lemon juice, sultanas, brandy, cinnamon, ground nutmeg and sugar if using, and mix to combine. Leave to rest for about 5 minutes then drain and scatter the apple slices and sultanas over one half of the base, leaving 2cm/¾in as a rim. Pull the uncovered half of dough up and over the filling and, using your fingers, crimp the edge to seal it forming a crescent shape. Prick the top once or twice with a fork, brush with the melted butter and sprinkle over the brown sugar.

3. Carefully transfer the baking parchment to a baking sheet and cook for about 15 minutes, or until golden and the base is cooked through. Allow to rest for a few minutes before serving with pouring cream.

Pear
pizza tatin

1 thin crust Sweet honey
pizza base (see page 16),
with the saffron omitted

800g/1lb 10oz pears, peeled,
cored and quartered

½ tsp Chinese 5 spice

130g/4½oz caster sugar

2 Tbsp butter

2 Tbsp cranberries (optional)

Handful of pecans

Makes 1 pizza

1. Preheat the oven to 180°C/350°F/Gas mark 4. Prepare the pizza base, rolling it out to approximately 25cm/10in in diameter and set aside.

2. In a large bowl toss the pear quarters with the Chinese 5 spice. Put the sugar in a 24cm/9½in diameter, 4.5cm/1¾in deep ovenproof frying pan. Scatter the butter over the sugar. Arrange pears in a snug circle around the pan, cut sides facing in the same direction. Tuck the remaining pears inside the circle. Scatter the cranberries and pecans between the pears. Heat the pan over medium – medium-high heat. Juices will bubble. Continue to cook, shaking the pan to loosen the contents every so often, until the juices have caramelized to a dark golden colour, about 30 minutes. Watch carefully so it doesn't burn. Remove from the heat, but leave contents in the pan.

3. Place the pizza base over the pears in the pan, tucking the edges of the base inside the pan. Bake for 10 minutes, cover with foil and bake for 15 minutes more. Invert the pan onto a serving platter. Cool slightly, slice and serve.

Date fudge

325g/11½oz butter
500g/1lb 2 oz plain flour
150g/5½oz caster sugar
1 tsp ground cinnamon
½ tsp cardamom
100g/3½ oz walnuts, halved
500g/1lb 2 oz pitted dates
1 tsp ground pistachio nuts

Serves 4

1. Melt the butter over a medium heat in a heavy-based saucepan. Add the flour, stirring constantly, until golden brown. Remove from the heat and cool slightly. Add the sugar, cinnamon and cardamom to the flour and butter and mix well.

2. Pour half the flour mixture into a flat 25cm/10in round dish and flatten the surface with the back of a spoon. Insert half a walnut inside each date and place the dates on top of the flour mixture. Cover the dates with the remaining flour mixture and again flatten the surface with the back of a spoon. Cut into diamond shapes. Sprinkle with ground pistachios and serve cold.

Baked apricots with bay leaves

750g/1½lb fresh apricots

300ml/10fl oz fruity red wine or unsweetened cranberry juice

60g/2oz light brown sugar

4 fresh bay leaves

To serve:

30g/1oz pecan halves, toasted and roughly chopped

Plain yogurt or pouring cream

Serves 6

1. Preheat the oven to 180°C/350°F/Gas mark 4. Wash the apricots and pat dry. Cut in half and remove the stones. Arrange the apricots neatly, cut-side up, in a shallow baking dish.

2. Pour over the red wine or juice and sprinkle the sugar over the fruit. Push the bay leaves in between the fruit and bake in the oven for about 1 hour until the fruit is tender and a rich red colour. Using a slotted spoon, remove the fruit from the juices and place in a heatproof dish.

3. Strain the cooking juices into a saucepan and bring to the boil. Cook for about 5 minutes until reduced and syrupy. Pour over the fruit and set aside to cool. Cover and chill for 2 hours before serving. To serve, sprinkle over the pecan nuts and serve with plain yogurt or pouring cream.

Bananas with honey and sesame seeds

55g/2oz sesame seeds

2 Tbsp runny honey

4 bananas, peeled and cut
in half

To serve:

Vanilla ice cream or Greek
yogurt

Serves 4

1. Heat a large frying pan or wok and add the sesame seeds. Toast them for about 30 seconds until browned, taking care not to burn them.

2. Add the honey and heat over a low heat until the honey is bubbling. Add the bananas and gently stir-fry for 30 seconds, making sure all the bananas are coated with the honey and sesame seeds. Serve with vanilla ice cream or thick Greek yogurt.

Chocolate brownies

100g/4oz butter

175g/6oz caster sugar

75g/3oz muscovado brown sugar

125g/4½ oz chocolate (plain or milk)

1 Tbsp golden syrup

2 eggs

1 tsp vanilla extract/essence

100g/4oz plain flour

2 Tbsp cocoa powder

½ tsp baking powder

Serves 4

1. Preheat the oven to 180°C/350°F/Gas mark 4. Put the butter, caster sugar, brown sugar, chocolate and golden syrup in a pan and melt gently on a low heat until smooth and lump-free. Remove the pan from the heat and allow to cool for 5–10 minutes.

2. Break the eggs into the small mixing bowl and whisk with the fork until light and frothy. Add the beaten eggs, vanilla extract, flour, baking powder and cocoa to the melted chocolate mixture and mix well.

3. Pour the mixture into the greased and lined cake tin and bake on the middle shelf of the oven for 20–25 minutes.

4. Remove from the oven and allow to cool for 20–30 minutes before cutting into squares.

Cherry clafoutis

90g/3oz plain flour

3 Tbsp caster sugar

½ tsp salt

4 eggs, beaten

300ml/10fl oz milk

150ml/5fl oz single cream

1 tsp vanilla extract

15g/½oz unsalted butter, softened

500g/1lb fresh cherries, stoned

Icing sugar, to dust

To serve:

Pouring cream (optional)

Serves 6

1. Preheat the oven to 190°C/375°F/Gas mark 5. Sift the flour, sugar and salt into a bowl and make a well in the centre. Add the eggs and pour in the milk and cream. Gradually work the flour into the eggs and milk and whisk to form a smooth, thick batter. Stir in the vanilla extract.

2. Grease a 25cm/10in round or shaped baking dish with the butter, add the cherries and pour the batter over them. Place the dish on a baking sheet and bake in the oven for about 45 minutes, until risen and golden – the middle should be just set. Serve warm, dusted with icing sugar and accompanied with pouring cream if liked.

Lemon meringue waffles

½ quantity Basic waffle
  batter (see page 27),
  sweetened
1 tsp finely grated lemon rind
6 Tbsp Greek yogurt
6 Tbsp lemon curd
6 small meringues, lightly
  crushed
Mint leaves, to decorate

Serves 6

1. Prepare the half quantity of waffle batter, adding
the lemon rind to the batter. Cook the waffles and keep
warm until you are ready to serve.

2. To serve, gently swirl the yogurt and lemon curd
together and spoon on top of the waffles. Sprinkle with
crushed meringue and decorate with mint leaves.

Lemon and sultana buttermilk pancakes

125g/4oz plain flour

2 tsp baking powder

½ tsp bicarbonate of soda

1 Tbsp caster sugar

2 eggs, separated

250ml/8fl oz buttermilk

Finely grated rind of 1 small
  lemon

60g/2oz sultanas

30g/1oz unsalted butter

To serve:

Plain yogurt

Maple syrup

Serves 4

1. Sift the flour, baking powder, bicarbonate of soda and sugar into a bowl. Make a well in the centre. Add the egg yolks, pour in the buttermilk and gradually work into the flour using a whisk. Beat until thick and smooth but don't over-mix.

2. In a grease-free bowl, whisk the egg whites until stiff and, using a large metal spoon, carefully fold into the batter together with the lemon rind and sultanas.

3. Heat a little butter in a large frying pan until bubbling, tilting the pan to coat the sides. Ladle 4 Tbsp batter into the pan to form a thick pancake about 10cm/4in in diameter. Cook over low to moderate heat for about 2½ minutes, until bubbles appear on the surface. Slide a palette knife under the pancake and flip. Brown the underside of the pancake for 2½ minutes. The pancake should puff up and thicken.

4. Turn the pancake out onto a wire rack lined with a clean tea towel and baking parchment. Fold the paper and towel over the pancake. Repeat to make eight pancakes. Re-butter the pan as necessary and stack the cooked pancakes between sheets of parchment. Serve with yogurt and maple syrup.

Coffee crêpes with caramel oranges

250g/8oz mascarpone

125g/4oz + 2 Tbsp caster
sugar

1 tsp vanilla extract

6 medium oranges

1 quantity Basic crêpe batter
(see page 25), sweetened

4 Tbsp cold espresso or
strong black coffee

Orange zest, to decorate

Serves 6

1. In a bowl, mix the mascarpone with 2 Tbsp sugar and the vanilla extract. Cover and chill until required.

2. Using a sharp knife, slice the top and bottom off the oranges. Slice off the peel taking away as much of the white pith as possible. Cut the oranges into thin slices and place in a shallow bowl. Cover and chill until required.

3. Prepare the batter, replacing 4 Tbsp milk with the cold espresso coffee. Cook the crêpes and keep warm until required.

4. Place the remaining sugar in a small saucepan and add 4 Tbsp water. Heat gently until dissolved and then increase the heat. Bring to the boil and boil for about 4 minutes until golden and caramelized. Remove from the heat and plunge the bottom of the pan into cold water to cease the cooking.

5. To serve, fill the crêpes with a generous spoonful of the mascarpone cheese and top with a few orange slices. Drizzle with caramel and quickly fold up. Serve decorated with orange zest.

Index

Almond and grape pastry 277

Apple, sultana and cinnamon strudel 281

Asparagus, bacon and cherry tomato pizza 133

Aubergine and okra curry 197

Baked apricots with bay leaves 287

Baked chicken legs 97

Balti vegetables with mango 205

Bananas with honey and sesame seeds 289

Barley risotto with roasted butternut squash and goat's cheese 213

Basic crêpe batter 25

Basic pancake batter 26

Basic savoury white sauce 24

Basic waffle batter 27

beef
  Chilli bean beef with nachos and cheese 115
  Five spice steak with peppers 113
  Marinated steak in tomato and wild mushroom sauce 117
  Spicy beef stir-fry 107
  Beef tomatoes stuffed with cheese and spinach 227
  Black bean and vegetable chilli with coriander-lime crème fraîche 225

blueberry
  Blueberry cheesecake ice cream 251
  Blueberry compôte 28

brochettes
  Mango and lamb brochettes 121
  Pork brochettes 75

Butternut squash soup with blue cheese and walnuts 43

Cajun hash browns with chorizo and cherry tomatoes 127

Capricciosa 135

Carrot and ginger soup 33

cheesecake
  Pear and ginger cheesecake 269
  Raspberry cheesecake 267

Cherry clafoutis 293

chicken
  Baked chicken legs 97
  Chicken biryani 95
  Chicken stock 18
  Chicken wings with coriander 101
  Coriander chicken on lemon grass skewers 77
  Kung Po chicken 89
  Lemon chicken stir-fry with cashew nuts 93
  Parmesan-coated chicken goujons with pesto dip 69
  Red pesto chicken with olives 91
  Very quick chicken curry 87

chickpea
  Chickpea and coriander cakes 239
  Chickpea and pimiento toasts 51
  Chickpea and sweetcorn cheese cakes 81
  Chickpea and tahini dip 83

Chilli bean beef with nachos and cheese 115

chocolate
  Chocolate banoffee pie 261
  Chocolate brownies 291
  Chocolate sugar syrup 29
  Dark chocolate ice cream 249
  White chocolate and berry pie 259

cod
  Cod and haddock fishcakes 145
  Cod provençal 167

Cod with chilli soy
vegetables 177
Coffee crêpes with caramel
oranges 299
coriander
Coriander chicken on lemon
grass skewers 77
Coriander pesto 21
Coriander pesto, prawn and
feta pizza 189
Crab and chilli rissoles 65
Creamy pork with mushrooms
and peppers 123
crêpes
Basic crêpe batter 24
Coffee crêpes with caramel
oranges 299
Spinach crêpes with mixed
mushrooms 241
Crispy pizza base 13
Crispy tuna with sweet chilli
vegetables 179
crostini
Mozzarella and roasted red
onion crostini 63
Mushroom crostini 67
Croûtons 21
curry
Aubergine and okra curry 197
Thai green vegetable curry 199
Very quick chicken curry 87
Custard sauce 29

Dark chocolate ice cream 249
Date fudge 285
Deep-dish apple pie 265

Egg pasta 17

Filo stuffed with nuts 279
Fish with tahini sauce and
walnuts 159
Five spice steak with peppers 113

Focaccia pizza base 15
French onion soup 47
Fresh lime tart 275
Fruit coulis 28

Gluten-free quick pizza base
dough 14
Gorgonzola and roasted red
onion pizza 221
Greek salad 245
Grilled garlic red mullet 147

Herbed potato pie 231

ice cream
Blueberry cheesecake ice
cream 251
Dark chocolate ice cream 249
Passionfruit sorbet 255
Tiramisu ice cream torta 257
Traditional rocky road
ice cream 253

Jambalaya pancakes 175

Kung Po chicken 89

Leek, fennel and basil tart 233
Lemon and sultana buttermilk
pancakes 297
Lemon chicken stir-fry with
cashew nuts 93
Lemon meringue waffles 295
Linguini with sweet onions and
Swiss chard 209

Mackerel salad 185
Mackerel with sweet and sour
plum relish 163
Make your own pizza party 137
mango
Balti vegetables with mango 205
Mango and lamb brochettes 121

Mango pudding 273
Prawns with mango 169
Marinated steak in tomato and
　wild mushroom sauce 117
Meat stock 18
Mediterranean fish stew 153
Melon and mint tea salad 271
Minted monkfish spiedini 157
Mixed vegetable curry 195
Moroccan vegetable tagine 203
Moussaka 109
Mozzarella and roasted red
　onion crostini 63
mushrooms
　Mushroom crostini 67
　Mushroom, wild rice and
　　ale pie 229
Mustard-spiced prawns and
　monkfish 141

Oven barbecued fish 187

Pad Thai with shredded
　omelette 99
pancakes
　Basic pancake batter 27
　Jambalaya pancakes 175
　Lemon and sultana buttermilk
　　pancakes 297
　Spinach pancakes with
　　haddock 161
Parmesan-coated chicken
　goujons with pesto dip 69
Passionfruit sorbet 255
Pasta carbonara 129
Patatas bravas 53
Pea and mint soup 35
Pear and ginger cheesecake 269
Pear pizza tatin 283
pizza
　Capricciosa 135
　Coriander pesto, prawn and
　　feta pizza 189

Crispy pizza base 13
Focaccia pizza base 15
Gluten-free quick pizza base
　dough 14
Gorgonzola and roasted red
　onion pizza 221
Make your own pizza party 137
Pear pizza tatin 283
Roasted red onion, artichoke
　and sage calzone 217
Rocket and new potato
　focaccia 219
Sweet honey pizza base 16
Walnut pesto and hot-smoked
　salmon pizza 173
Walnut pesto, aubergine and
　pomegranate pizza 223
Plum duck with stir-fried
　vegetables 131
Poached rhubarb with ginger
　cake 263
Poppy seed waffles with
　ratatouille 243
Pork brochettes 75
Prawn bruschetta with garlic 59
Prawn croquettes 79
Prawns with mango 169
Prawns with minted chilli and
　orange sauce 151
pumpkin
　Pumpkin and sage pilaf 201
　Pumpkin ravioli with sage and
　　pine nut butter 211

Quick classic tomato sauce 24
Quick kedgeree 183
Quick scone base 14

Raspberry cheesecake 267
Red pesto chicken with olives 91
Red-braised fillets of sea bass 171
Roasted mixed peppers on
　toast 61

Cod with chilli soy
vegetables 177
Coffee crêpes with caramel
oranges 299
coriander
Coriander chicken on lemon
grass skewers 77
Coriander pesto 21
Coriander pesto, prawn and
feta pizza 189
Crab and chilli rissoles 65
Creamy pork with mushrooms
and peppers 123
crêpes
Basic crêpe batter 24
Coffee crêpes with caramel
oranges 299
Spinach crêpes with mixed
mushrooms 241
Crispy pizza base 13
Crispy tuna with sweet chilli
vegetables 179
crostini
Mozzarella and roasted red
onion crostini 63
Mushroom crostini 67
Croûtons 21
curry
Aubergine and okra curry 197
Thai green vegetable curry 199
Very quick chicken curry 87
Custard sauce 29

Dark chocolate ice cream 249
Date fudge 285
Deep-dish apple pie 265

Egg pasta 17

Filo stuffed with nuts 279
Fish with tahini sauce and
walnuts 159
Five spice steak with peppers 113

Focaccia pizza base 15
French onion soup 47
Fresh lime tart 275
Fruit coulis 28

Gluten-free quick pizza base
dough 14
Gorgonzola and roasted red
onion pizza 221
Greek salad 245
Grilled garlic red mullet 147

Herbed potato pie 231

ice cream
Blueberry cheesecake ice
cream 251
Dark chocolate ice cream 249
Passionfruit sorbet 255
Tiramisu ice cream torta 257
Traditional rocky road
ice cream 253

Jambalaya pancakes 175

Kung Po chicken 89

Leek, fennel and basil tart 233
Lemon and sultana buttermilk
pancakes 297
Lemon chicken stir-fry with
cashew nuts 93
Lemon meringue waffles 295
Linguini with sweet onions and
Swiss chard 209

Mackerel salad 185
Mackerel with sweet and sour
plum relish 163
Make your own pizza party 137
mango
Balti vegetables with mango 205
Mango and lamb brochettes 121

Mango pudding 273
Prawns with mango 169
Marinated steak in tomato and
    wild mushroom sauce 117
Meat stock 18
Mediterranean fish stew 153
Melon and mint tea salad 271
Minted monkfish spiedini 157
Mixed vegetable curry 195
Moroccan vegetable tagine 203
Moussaka 109
Mozzarella and roasted red
    onion crostini 63
mushrooms
    Mushroom crostini 67
    Mushroom, wild rice and
        ale pie 229
Mustard-spiced prawns and
    monkfish 141

Oven barbecued fish 187

Pad Thai with shredded
    omelette 99
pancakes
    Basic pancake batter 27
    Jambalaya pancakes 175
    Lemon and sultana buttermilk
        pancakes 297
    Spinach pancakes with
        haddock 161
Parmesan-coated chicken
    goujons with pesto dip 69
Passionfruit sorbet 255
Pasta carbonara 129
Patatas bravas 53
Pea and mint soup 35
Pear and ginger cheesecake 269
Pear pizza tatin 283
pizza
    Capricciosa 135
    Coriander pesto, prawn and
        feta pizza 189

Crispy pizza base 13
Focaccia pizza base 15
Gluten-free quick pizza base
    dough 14
Gorgonzola and roasted red
    onion pizza 221
Make your own pizza party 137
Pear pizza tatin 283
Roasted red onion, artichoke
    and sage calzone 217
Rocket and new potato
    focaccia 219
Sweet honey pizza base 16
Walnut pesto and hot-smoked
    salmon pizza 173
Walnut pesto, aubergine and
    pomegranate pizza 223
Plum duck with stir-fried
    vegetables 131
Poached rhubarb with ginger
    cake 263
Poppy seed waffles with
    ratatouille 243
Pork brochettes 75
Prawn bruschetta with garlic 59
Prawn croquettes 79
Prawns with mango 169
Prawns with minted chilli and
    orange sauce 151
pumpkin
    Pumpkin and sage pilaf 201
    Pumpkin ravioli with sage and
        pine nut butter 211

Quick classic tomato sauce 24
Quick kedgeree 183
Quick scone base 14

Raspberry cheesecake 267
Red pesto chicken with olives 91
Red-braised fillets of sea bass 171
Roasted mixed peppers on
    toast 61

Roasted red onion, artichoke
and sage calzone 217
Rocket and new potato
focaccia 219
Rocket pesto 20
Root vegetable and winter
herb cakes 237

salmon
Salmon and herb waffles 165
Salmon fish fingers with pea and
potato mash 191
Salmon steamed with lemon
grass, lime and basil 155
Salmon with sun-blush
tomatoes 143
Salmon, dill and fresh pea
pasta 181
Samosas 71
Smoked fish chowder 45
Spaghetti bolognaise 119
Spanish omelette 55
Spicy beef stir-fry 107
Spicy sweetcorn patties 235
Spinach crêpes with mixed
mushrooms 241
Spinach pancakes with
haddock 161
Spring vegetable and pancetta
soup 39
Stuffed mussels 57
Stuffed vegetables 111
Sweet and sour brown tamarind
chutney 22
Sweet honey pizza base 16
Sweet red pepper and oregano
soup 49

Tagliatelle with caramelized
onions and walnuts 207
Tamarind purée 19
Thai chilli paste 23
Thai green vegetable curry 199

Tiramisu ice cream torta 257
tomato
Tomato fritters 73
Tomato soup 37
Tomato, black olive, garlic and
basil salsa 22
Traditional rocky road
ice cream 253
tuna
Crispy tuna with sweet chilli
vegetables 179
Tuna and bean salad 149
turkey
Turkey burgers with cranberry
relish 103
Turkey meatballs in a rich tomato
sauce 105
Tuscan bean soup 41

Vegetable stock 19
Very quick chicken curry 87

waffles
Basic waffle batter 29
Lemon meringue waffles 295
Poppy seed waffles with
ratatouille 243
Salmon and herb waffles 165
Walnut pesto 20
Walnut pesto and hot-smoked
salmon pizza 173
Walnut pesto, aubergine and
pomegranate pizza 223
Warm pasta salad 125
White chocolate and berry pie 259
White onion paste 23
Wild mushroom and Parmesan
risotto 215

Acknowledgments

Our thanks to:

Catherine Atkinson; pp. 6–12, 129, 191

Abigail Brown and Melissa Webb; pp. 41, 49, 59, 63, 69, 73, 157, 149, 77

Pat Chapman; pp. 65, 71, 97, 141, 147, 169, 195, 227

Pippa Cuthbert and Lindsay Cameron-Wilson; pp. 33, 35, 37, 39, 45, 47, 43, 61, 197, 233, 229, 239, 225, 211, 203, 213, 209, 133, 135, 137, 173, 189, 219, 221, 223, 283, 217, 281, 249, 251, 253, 255, 257

Tomas Garcia; pp. 75, 79, 55, 53, 51

Fiona Hamilton-Fairley; pp. 119, 125, 291

Kathryn Hawkins; pp. 81, 161, 165, 175, 241, 243, 297, 299, 295, 293, 103, 121, 275, 267, 263, 271, 287, 265, 277, 269, 163, 259, 261

Maria Khalife; pp. 57, 101, 185, 245, 109, 83, 95, 111, 159, 187, 285, 279, 273

Katie Rogers; pp. 87, 107, 93, 143, 177, 179, 181, 183, 201, 207, 289

Joy Skipper; pp. 67, 231

Wendy Sweetser; pp. 123, 89, 91, 113, 131, 105, 115, 117, 99, 127, 145, 151, 153, 155, 167, 171, 215, 205, 235, 237, 199